waterside
living

RYLAND
PETERS
& SMALL

LONDON NEW YORK

waterside living

inspirational homes by lakes, rivers and the sea

LESLIE GEDDES-BROWN

PHOTOGRAPHY BY JAN BALDWIN

For this edition:
Designer Carl Hodson
Senior editor Henrietta Heald
Production Paul Harding
Art director Anne-Marie Bulat
Editorial director Julia Charles
Publishing director Alison Starling

Stylist Sylvie Jones

First published in the United Kingdom in 2001
This paperback edition published in 2006
by Ryland Peters & Small
20–21 Jockey's Fields
London WC1R 4BW
www.rylandpeters.com
10 9 8 7 6 5 4 3 2 1

Text © Leslie Geddes-Brown 2001, 2006
Design and photographs © Ryland Peters & Small
2001, 2006

ISBN-10 1-84597-153-1
ISBN-13 978-1-84597-153-3

A CIP record for this book is available from
the British Library.

Printed and bound in China.

CONTENTS

INTRODUCTION

I feel well qualified to write on waterside living. For more than a decade I have lived in a house encircled by a moat that at its widest measures 15 metres from bank to bank. Two sides of the house, which dates from 1390, rise directly from the water. Eric Sandon, writing about the old houses of Suffolk, says it has 'the look of a vessel at anchor'.

So I do know about the pleasures of living with the ripples lapping outside my dining room, reflected on my kitchen ceiling, and the ducks, moorhens and coots cruising past the open window where we sit on warm evenings. We can see our group of golden orfe swimming barely below the surface and, gliding just above the surface, the swallows, house martins and swifts that visit us from Africa every summer. They love the water, which draws the flies. It also attracts dragonflies resembling small helicopters and water voles that busy themselves along the banks.

I also know something of the problems of waterside living since I was brought up in the low-lying city of York in the north of England. My father was a doctor there and, at least once, had to visit his sick patients by horse and cart or, if they were nearer the River Ouse, by rowing boat. We lived with the constant risk that we, too, would be flooded – it never happened because our house was on a main road 200 metres from the river, but we became attuned to the regular alarms. Fed by numerous tributaries in the Yorkshire dales, the Ouse was a dangerous flow, regularly sweeping away reckless young men who dived in after a night at one of the waterside pubs.

Yet, even with the risk of flooding, once you have discovered the delights of waterside living, you never want to go away again. The attraction is the constant change, as I found out while staying at Brantwood, the house of Victorian art critic John Ruskin, which overlooks Coniston Water in the Lake District. Every day, every hour, every minute brought variations in the clouds, the atmosphere and the light that played over the lake and the crag known as the Old Man of Coniston, which brooded over the water on the opposite shore. I have therefore been delighted to discover that the owners of the houses featured in this book have found pleasures from their waterside existence as equally diverse as those I get from mine. We all, it seems, have something different to enjoy.

the essence of
waterside living

It must have been early in civilization's history when water changed from being a mere security feature to a source of pure pleasure. According to legend, Venice was founded on 25 March 421, at midday exactly. No doubt the first colonizers sought out the lagoon with its hundreds of tiny isles as a place of safety. It was hard for raiders to find their way around the marshes and inlets, which the residents knew by heart. But the Venetians soon began to adore their damp bog of a hideaway. Even today, years after the decline of 'La Serenissima', we can see how they gave their city gifts of jewels and statues, and carved wellheads and built houses so ornate that they look like iced cakes rising from the murky canals. Artists were enchanted by the light that comes from the combination of water, marble and sun, and which, to this day, make Venice the most painted city in the world. It is also among the most visited cities and one perfectly attuned to romance.

It was the desire for security that led people to dig moats around their houses – but how the water enhances the buildings. Look at the Loire chateaux with their stone walls rising from still sheets of water. Look at the vernacular buildings of England that are moated and full of charm. My area of Suffolk has more moats than any other part of Britain – at least 568, of which about 200 are linked with ancient halls.

Castles were also moated against marauders (cattle thieves and bands of brigands rather than armies) or perched on cliffs and plugs of rock directly above the sea, or on peninsulas in Scottish lochs.

Before I had my own waterside retreat, the place where I most wanted to live was Lindisfarne Castle on Holy Island, off England's north-east coast, converted into a house by Sir Edwin Lutyens at the start of the 20th century. It was the combination of the wild Northumbrian seas that lash this historic island, with its past of Viking raids, and the comfort that Lutyens had built into the interior through massive stone walls, narrow windows and great welcoming fires that seemed irresistibly attractive.

Waterside living often has an element of danger about it – the lash of storms that make landfall on your cliffs, the driving rain and howling winds that keen around the house, the risk of flooding and

drowning. On a dark winter's night, as the gales intensify, I wouldn't be anywhere other than in my moat room in front of a log fire big enough to take tree trunks or in the four-poster bed upstairs in a room which jetties out over the water so I can see its white horses through the floor beneath my feet.

The ancient Egyptians created ornamental water features in their gardens some 4000 years ago, as did the Moors in Spain as long ago as AD 900. Both the Taj Mahal, with its canals reflecting the white-marble building, and the Palace of Versailles, with its spurting fountains and curvaceous ponds, were created then. There was no added spice of danger in these elegant watery gardens – they were built for grandeur and the contemplation of manmade beauty.

Gradually, as security became less important, the adventurous and the rich went in search of water in all its dramatic forms. The Grand Tour, all the rage in the 18th century, saw rich young gentlemen from northern Europe travel to the classical lands in search of excitement, education and booty. Their adventures took them down the Rhine, sampling the hock and not liking it much, and admiring the craggy, impregnable castles that the robber barons built to take tolls from the travellers who crossed Germany by boat.

The tourists arrived in Italy via the Alps with their snow-covered peaks and still mountain lakes, or took the easy way – a boat to Genoa. Then they would progress through Italy admiring the scenery – the Arno bisecting Florence, the Tiber winding through the ruins of Rome, the lakes of Como and Garda – before reaching Naples. 'See Naples and die' summed up the romantic views on offer there. There was Vesuvius, erupting throughout the 18th and 19th centuries; Pompeii and Herculaneum, which had recently been uncovered from volcanic debris; the wonderful villas along the Bay of Naples itself; and the Aeolian islands and Sicily. Grand tourists swarmed to Sicily to see the Greek temples of Paestum. They visited the island of Capri, where the Emperor Tiberius had earlier discovered his own enjoyment of waterside living, and they admired the volcanoes of Etna and Stromboli.

Along with the milordi came quantities of artists from France and England, eager to capture the seascapes of the cities along with the torrents which

crashed down the slopes of the Alps and the famous
lakes and the resorts beside them. Artists such as
Thomas Jones, Francis Towne and Alexander Cozens
captured the picturesque but controlled wilderness of
Italy which, in turn, led to the 19th-century craze for
the Romantic in Britain. If the rich could make the
trek to the Mediterranean, the middle classes could
take their coaches – and, later, trains – up to the Lake
District, the Black Mountains of Wales and the Scottish
Highlands. Intrepid Victorian ladies visited the Alps
and climbed the Matterhorn in their crinolines, while
Queen Victoria herself took a boat down the Rhine.
This was the era when poets flocked to Windermere
and Ullswater to be inspired by lowering mountains
and the dark lakes beneath; when painters travelled
over the borders to capture Snowdon and Betws-y-
Coed as the bracken turned amber, and put up easels
on Scottish hillsides to picture the deer drinking at
the side of Loch Lomond or mysterious Loch Ness.

Queen Victoria, seduced by the romance of the
Highlands, decreed that Balmoral should be built for
her summer holidays – and established a tradition kept
up by the British Royal Family ever since. Encouraged
by Victoria's enthusiasm for all things Scottish, rich
industrialists rented fishing lodges beside the great
trout and salmon rivers of the Spey and Dee or flocked
to the islands. Arran became a resort and the Duke of
Buccleuch built a castle on Bute. Islands have been
romantic ever since.

I myself have had a long love affair with islands.
However small they are, they seem complete. On the
tiny island of Pantelleria, once a prison for Italian
fascists, I met my first olive trees while scrambling
down the cliffs to the sea. A young carabiniere, in his
smart uniform, climbed up and picked me a branch,
complete with infant olives. On the beach the
fishermen cooked their own sardines with a touch of
local olive oil on portable barbecues. On Ischia I
visited the composer Sir William Walton, whose wife
has created extraordinary gardens around their cliffside
villa, and on Elba I saw the little villa where Napoleon
spent his first years of captivity. Tobago, a tiny island
in the West Indies almost completely devoted to
pleasure, allowed me to lie on its soft white beaches
with whispering palm trees looking impossibly like

a tourist poster. Tuna lurked under wooden piers, waiting to be caught and grilled for lunch. During breakfast by the beach, minute hummingbirds would come to suck sweetness from the tropical flowers.

If the 19th century was the time of romantic lakes and islands, the 20th was the time when beaches and swimming were invented. The travel writer Eric Newby describes the palatial hotels that were built along the Riviera from 1912 onwards. They were designed 'for the reception of royalty, which included whole squads of grand dukes (sightings of a dozen at a time were not uncommon; they used to come for the weekend from St Petersburg in special trains), noblemen, statesmen and millionaires'. They came 'to play at the casinos and be given the kiss of life by such *grandes horizontales* as La Belle Otero, Gaby Deslys and Liane de Pouget'.

The Victorians may have stripped off in wheeled carts dragged by donkeys into the sea, but it was not until the era of Coco Chanel that it was smart to lounge in chic palazzo pyjamas on the Riviera. King Edward VIII went on a scandalous cruise with Mrs Simpson, and the Carlton Hotel in Cannes suggested to the Aga Khan that they should bottle his bath water and sell it to the faithful.

After the First World War, Gerald and Sara Murphy – two rich Americans transformed by F. Scott Fitzgerald into characters in his novel *Tender is the Night* – discovered La Garoupe while staying with Cole Porter at Cap d'Antibes. Very few people went to the Riviera in the summer then or bathed in the sea. Gerald Murphy wrote, 'We dug out a corner of the beach and bathed there and sat in the sun, and we decided that this was where we wanted to be.'

They had invented a whole new way of life – one that attracted Picasso, writers such as Somerset Maugham, Ernest Hemingway and Françoise Sagan, and film directors such as Roger Vadim – which was to last until travel and the beautiful life became the property of ordinary tourists and, therefore, less worth having.

The tiny coastal village of Portofino was all the rage with 1950s Hollywood stars such as Rex Harrison and Errol Flynn, who misbehaved at the Hotel Splendido, and, shortly after, Brigitte Bardot turned an unpopular fishing village called St Tropez into a resort that still attracts the rich and famous. Suntans were de rigueur,

bikinis were essential, and seaside hedonism was the envy of all those people who were unable to afford the outrageous prices.

The modernist architects of the 20th century – Le Corbusier, Frank Lloyd Wright and the Bauhaus group – created a style that was perfect for the waterside. Since it was now possible to make plate glass in huge sheets, and since central heating and air conditioning were becoming standard, houses could be made to embrace dramatic views. They could be given glass walls from floor to ceiling, and overhanging balconies and verandas to make good views spectacular.

Though these dramatically open, flat-roofed houses stormed over California, with its miles of wonderful Pacific cliffs and beaches, they proved less attractive on the east coast of America, where the WASP bankers and politicians began to colonize the Hamptons, Martha's Vineyard and Long Island. Holiday homes there were strictly vernacular: weatherboarded, sash-windowed and, towards the end of the 20th century, full of American country antiques and found objects.

Curiously, as the 20th century moved on, the west coast's love of waterside modernism grew more exotic and tropical, while the east coast's style and that of England have merged. So there is Ralph Lauren in New York celebrating very English classic clothes in very English gardens, while in England waterside houses espouse Shaker styles and American duck decoys. We have adopted many of Nancy Lancaster's formidably foresighted ideas in English country houses, while modern-day stars such as Tommy Hilfiger have hired Colefax and Fowler.

At the other side of the world, Australia is turning its back on British influences in favour of the Bauhaus and Lloyd Wright Cubist approach. Recently, this has been one of the most innovatively artistic countries in the world, and that goes for architecture as much as literature and gardening. And the country has some of the most beautiful and wild settings on offer. How many of us can enjoy the luxury of living on an island without any roads yet go to work each day in a city as vibrant as Sydney?

Fashions come and go – look what has happened to suntans – but great cities such as Stockholm, San Francisco and Sydney have always been built at

strategic points. There are few that are not built on rivers, around safe harbours or at key ocean-crossing points. Just as the Scottish islands were less remote 200 years ago than they are now, because all traffic was waterborne, the people who sited cities in history were well aware that water was the source of life. Iron Age forts and besieged castles could hold out on hills for a limited time but, without water, impregnability was dangerous.

Many of the town houses most in demand are still those with river views. If you can look out over the Seine or the Hudson, the Rhine or the Thames, you will have paid a premium for your position. Similarly, those who can see the harbour and sea around San Francisco or the world-famous opera house and bridge in Sydney can reckon that they own some of the most famous vistas the world can offer.

Stockholm, like Venice, seems all about water, but the light there is cooler and more steely. Its colourful houses are reflected in the harbour waters, and the fish market is a foodie's dream. From Stockholm the Swedes take boats to other islands for long, lazy summer holidays. In their short sunny season they have perfected the art of waterside living, with small, familiar boathouses and summer houses built directly on the water, each with windows opening onto the ideal view. Interiors are left simple and friendly, with only the softest watery colours on walls and furniture.

Many of the rest of us yearn for the natural sea-washed pebble rather than the hewn block of stone; we have rediscovered the magic of the patterns of seashells and coral, which were last so lovingly admired in the 16th century. We have turned our backs on electric light in favour of candles – at least when convenient – and we long for moonlight on water and reflected sunlight rippling on the ceiling. Where we can, we find homes unaffected by artificial light at night, places where we can see the stars and hear the seabirds as they nest on the cliffs.

As we have found, water is an elemental force. Try to harness it and it evades you; try to force it to your will and it defeats you. In a synthetic world, water is still the great force of nature. Yes, it's dangerous. Yes, it's unpredictable. And yes, it's untameable too. That is, of course, why we value it so much.

lakeside living

No continent can boast of the grandeur of its lakes with more confidence than North America – and among those who live by the lakes a culture has evolved that owes much to the Native Americans, early pioneers, fishermen and trappers.

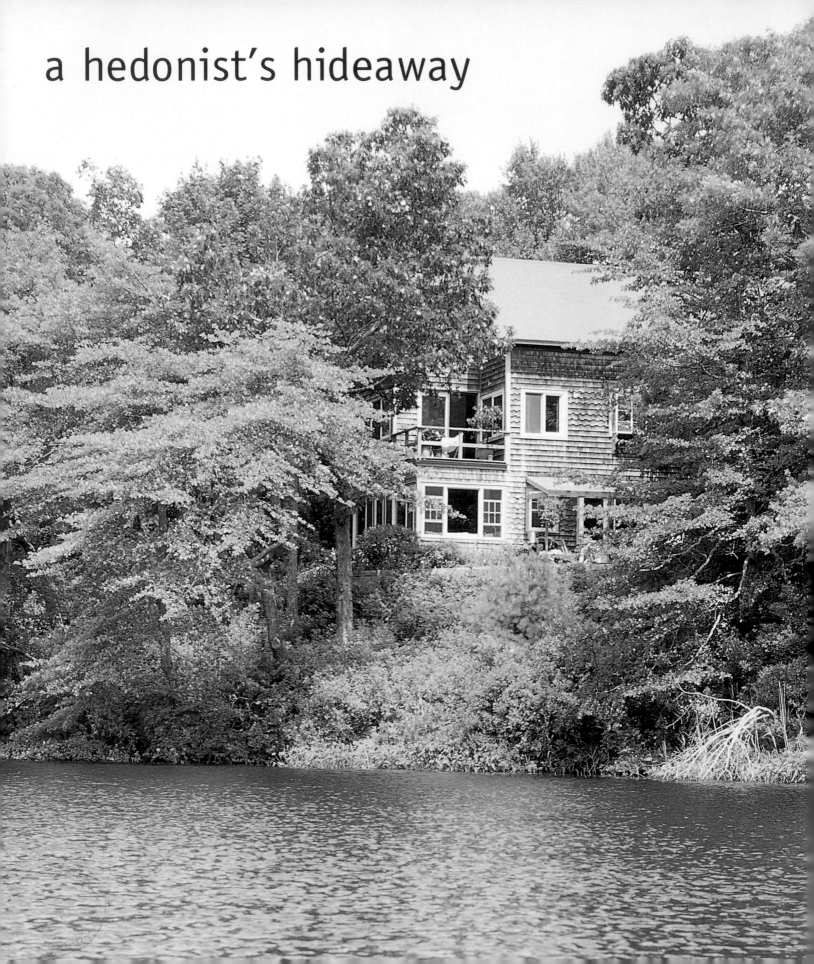

a hedonist's hideaway

Devoted to the pursuit of fun and relaxation after hard work, this charming shingled cottage is a potent fantasy come true.

Difficult though it may be to believe today, there was a time when nobody had heard of the Hamptons. Instead of being thronged with the beautiful people weekending their cares away after a long hard stint in New York City, the area was covered by potato fields stretching as far as the eye could see. That was before the idea of detox for body and soul became fashionable – before the rich and stressed gave themselves a dose of medicine in the form of a weekend of picnicking, sailing and strolling by the ocean. Today the area is very different.

Fern Mallis, an executive director of the Council of Fashion Designers of America, wanted her own slice of the Hamptons, but she turned her back on the sea and found a site on a freshwater lake. 'Every estate agent will tell you about this farmer or that who'll never sell his fields, he's had them for 150 years. The next thing you know, you look out the kitchen window and there are 18 houses going up. But you can't build on a lake.'

Despite the demand for building plots, this is still agricultural land. 'There are farms all over the place, growing corn, tomatoes, potatoes, squash, pumpkins and seasonal vegetables. The earth is very fertile on the "east end" and everything grows, from pine trees to every conceivable flowering plant.'

During her working week in New York, Fern may go to three parties a night, four nights in a row. So weekends by the water, with not a concrete tower or a cocktail bar in sight, are an essential tool of the job – even though she can't quite bring herself to turn off the fax machine as well as the phone.

Like many other owners of waterside homes, Fern's love affair started long ago. She bought the charming shingled cottage in 1996, but only after staying for several summers on the shores of the same lake. Fern acted throughout as her own architect, designer, decorator and general contractor. You can tell why she's a top executive from her attitude to the work:

RIGHT, BELOW AND OPPOSITE The exterior of Fern Mallis's Hampton house, shingled and painted white, is infinitely welcoming, with large verandas, windows scattered throughout and a series of paths and steps leading up from the jetty and the moored canoe at the water's edge. The garden is so densely wooded that, from the water, the house seems to peep out through the canopy of leaves.

'I removed several walls and I had to replace many windows, lay tile flooring, gut the kitchen and install a new one – all of which is open and user-friendly, as weekend houses are all about entertaining, eating and making it all accessible. It was so exciting.'

She began to plan the transformation even before the ink on the contract was dry. 'I'd decorated the house ten times in my head already.' She started by removing a lot of wood panelling, which had made the rooms very dark, and painted the rooms white instead. The views towards the lake were opened up, and the kitchen became part of the main downstairs room.

One of the principal attractions of the lakeside and the Hamptons is the quality of the light, which Fern has tried hard to introduce into the house. 'The Hamptons is a very special place. It is both country and beach community at the same time. The natural "east end" light is unique to the area, and the reason why painters have traditionally worked and lived there – Willem de Kooning, Jackson Pollock, Eric Fischl, Ross Bleckner and many more.'

The cottage itself dictated the style that Fern chose. 'I decorated it as it is because the house has a certain spirit and attitude. While I generally prefer hard-edged modern interiors, this is clearly a country house, with shingles, window panes, wood floors and moulding.' Nevertheless, the rooms offer a monochromatic feel throughout, probably as a result of the stark white of the walls and the preponderance of huge windows, their frames also painted white, shaded with Venetian

'The sunsets are brilliant. The air is clean and clear. One can smell and hear the ocean, and the beaches are some of the widest, longest and most beautiful on the East Coast.'

THIS PICTURE, INSET AND FAR LEFT, SMALL PICTURES
Life by the lake consists of far more than just a glimpse of water from the windows. The decor around the rooms and windows should evoke what is outside: an old Chinese lantern, a boat-shaped dish filled with bright green apples and pears and a colourful cushion all have this effect. Meanwhile, a corner of the living area uses the simplest monochromes and rattan furniture to draw attention to the windows and their view beyond. Even the rug and the stained floor are kept as plain as can be.

FAR LEFT, ABOVE Fern has created an informal atmosphere by refusing to make everything match. In this part of the living room, for example, there are strongly shaped modern chairs teamed with deep comfortable sofas, both upholstered in white.

ABOVE The colours of the log pile and potting shed look supremely natural, as does an old woven-wood chair – but such simplicity is achieved only with guile.

ABOVE RIGHT AND LEFT The skills involved in decorating these luscious homes include knowing when to use colour and when to avoid it. Fern Mallis loves the natural colours of flowers, fruit and vegetables. Here she has arranged watermelon slices on a black-and-white dish set on a table covered with the bright primary colours of the American flag. This provides the only bright spot in a garden vista (left), where a leaning branch frames a glimpse of the table among the hydrangeas with the lake shimmering beyond.

blinds. Elsewhere she has created an informal atmosphere by bringing together pieces that do not match. For example, dining-room chairs can be wickerwork with arms, country wooden chairs with hard seats and white cushions, or wooden armchairs with drop-in white seats. They cluster around a heavy wooden farm table covered in charming and casual baskets and sisal holders full of local gourds, herbs and arrays of votive candles for the evening.

Upstairs, the decorative style is what Fern describes as 'English/British/Moroccan' – even though her bedroom contains a typically American half-tester bed in dark wood with heavily turned poles. The room has a tiny veranda and, because it is at the corner of the house, offers views over two different stretches of water. She has given it a small sitting area all of its own with a pretty round table piled with curvaceous Moorish boxes of wood and metal. There's a kilim under the table, and old kilims have been made into cushion covers. The floors in this room are stained white beech, adding even more light to the combined reflections of sun and water.

The care taken over the detailing of the floors in each room gives the house its unique flavour. In the entrance hall, where visitors are introduced to Fern's love of collecting, the floor is a deep reddish black. There is a row of tiny chairs, made both for children and as apprentice pieces, and a whole series of fern specimens, all lime-green fronds and deep-cut silhouettes. The nearly black planking runs through into the open-plan living area, where floor rugs take up the monochrome scheme. This is further emphasized by a series of black-and-white striped bowls, which she also collects. All the snatches of colour come from incidentals, making it possible to change the feeling of a room entirely between summer and winter. Towards the end of the summer there are vases of brilliant yellow sunflowers, posies of daisies and large bowls filled with nothing but foliage. Vegetables are used to equally good

for the weekend or every day. 'I stained the floors dark and covered much of the furniture in white. I bought a lot of pieces in the country at various places, looking out for different woods that were both warm and appropriate. The house is accessorized with my huge miniature chair collection, kilim pillows, ikat pillows, Picasso print pillows, cashmere and other throws. All of it is about being comfortable, lying back, reading, watching endless movies on TV or, in summer, sitting outside and enjoying the lake and the sun. All the paintings are by my dad, my sisters or my nieces.'

The garden is as important in this scheme as the house. It, too, is meant to evoke long-gone summers, relaxation, parties and fun. Paths and steps lead down through dense woodland to the lake and its old wooden jetty with a moored canoe. There are areas where sawn logs are stored for winter fires and where old-fashioned terracotta pots sit on shelves waiting to be planted with summer-blooming scented flowers. Everywhere there are American classic chairs made of curved branches and bleached by the sun, or of painted planks reclined for maximum comfort.

There is nothing here that will not give pleasure. Anything ugly is banned, as is anything work-related. 'I get more joy out of two days here on a weekend than I ever knew possible,' says Fern. 'Just watching the water and the way the sun or moon reflect on the surface, the wind or the ice in winter. I can stare at it for hours and never be bored. I feel as if my batteries are recharged just by being here – and my batteries do get depleted by a typical work week. I enjoy being here all year around, to watch and feel the seasons change, to sleep late and do nothing. To be here and see many friends. Or to be here and see no one.'

ABOVE The main bedroom has fine views over the lake, whose fleeting colours are enhanced by the monochrome shades of the room, with its colonial half-tester bed and stained beech floor. The set of library steps provides a means of climbing up onto the bed should jumping fail.

OPPOSITE The owner has succeeded in evoking the colours of the land outside in her collection of ferny botanical specimens – just one of her passions. Another passion is tiny children's and apprentice chairs.

RIGHT All the colours in the kitchen area come from the bright vegetables and flowers, along with the brightly striped cushions made from folded fabrics.

effect – with, for example, yellow tomatoes arranged in the black-and-white bowls, or fresh green and yellow sweetcorn in a natural basket.

Cushions and throws are another device to add splashes of colour. Scarlet oriental-style throws are casually draped over the half-tester bed, and striped fabrics act as cushions on the high chairs around the kitchen counter. In summer, even the outside wooden jetty is adorned with a bright mixture of coloured fabrics, which look artlessly beautiful when seen from above, from the upper rooms. An American flag drapes an outdoor dining table, with shockingly clashing pink watermelon slices above its scarlet stripes.

Fern's intention is to emphasize the qualities of the house while making the decor ideal for entertaining and relaxing. When you hear her speak about what she is trying to achieve – what she does achieve – it creates a potent fantasy, redolent of the atmosphere that we are all trying to create in our homes, whether

serenity in the forest

In a remote part of Maine teeming with moose and bear, birds and fish, a house constructed by hand with spruce logs from the nearby forest stands serenely on the shores of a long lake.

It is hard for Europeans to understand that there are still virtually unexplored areas of wilderness in the USA. There are huge lakes, acres of dense forest and towering mountains that were once the hunting grounds of Native Americans and later the solitary preserves of trappers and pioneer farmers.

Paul and Melba Chodosh found their own wilderness just after the Second World War. It is a full day's drive from their Manhattan apartment but that doesn't deter them. Based in New York all winter, they pine for its solitude and long for the spring to bring them back.

Their holding is in Maine on the shores of a long lake. 'It's been a long love affair,' says Mel. They first found the area in 1946, and went back regularly until, in 1960, they bought their first house, or 'camp' as they call it. Three years after that they bought a second camp, and this has been their family home ever since.

The house was built in the early 20th century by hand from logs of spruce – which were also peeled by hand and put into place with a pulley, horses and manpower. 'The builder would have lived alone there, in what was a one-room log cabin with a well and a

sink. He was a French Canadian and clearly a good designer because the plan was great. He later built two or three other houses for people who lived here in the hunting and fishing season. It must have been a hard life because it gets extremely cold in winter: −30°F (−34°C). The lake freezes solid; there's a hotel nearby that still cuts ice from the lake to cool the icehouse where they store food. There was only liquor and wood stoves to keep them warm, and we know the French Canadian died poor and a drunk. He never enjoyed the benefits of his work and talent.'

This house has seen the arrival of the Chodoshes' five children, their children's spouses and, latterly, their 11 grandchildren and two step-grandchildren. 'It's a focal point for family gatherings, children, husbands, wives and their children. It's a major part of our lives.' Since Paul retired as a surgeon in New York 12 years ago, they have spent more time here than ever. Recently, the couple hired the architect Stephen Blatt to enlarge their holding and, to Mel's relief, increase the kitchen size.

Blatt explains what was behind the changes: 'After 30 years of benign, respectful nurturing of the six original buildings, the family initially sought help to renovate the kitchen. Mel, a gourmet cook, wanted a facility better equipped than the original "summer" kitchen, better integrated with the house, with views to the lake and a place to eat and schmooze in rare moments with no guests or family in tow. This "small project" became an adventure in architectural "neo-archaeology" as we proceeded together looking at the entire house, then the entire compound.'

So the whole kitchen was moved and made bigger, while the old kitchen became a studio where Mel works as a potter. 'The new, enlarged, reorientated kitchen is

THIS PICTURE The family have known the waters of this huge and unpopulated lake in Maine since 1946. They bought their second 'camp' there in 1963.

LEFT, ABOVE AND BELOW The main house dates from about 1900, and has recently had a formal staircase to the door and veranda added. It is one of six buildings that made up the original property. The sauna, which also has a wonderful view of the lake, is built of rough logs like the house. A 'no hunting' sign is not simply a joke: hunting is strictly controlled in the area.

'We tried to make the additions fit in with the original house and to look as though they had always been there.'

LEFT Wood is the main fuel out in these forests, and along with open fires the house has wood-burning stoves, like this one in the sauna overlooking the lake.

THIS PAGE AND INSET PAGE 30 Mel is a potter, and her bowls, put on tables with tiles also made by her, are filled with colourful fruit. A cut-tin lantern casts shadows on the wall at night.

more accessible from the driveway, to the dining room and other support spaces,' says Blatt. 'This new kitchen generated a new scheme through the house, including a new front door, mudroom, laundry room and office. A guest room was tucked above along a support spine, lined floor to ceiling with bookshelves.'

Mel simply finds that there is now a lot more space. Where once her children would perch on the worktops, there is now room for everything. 'I had great pleasure in planning the kitchen. It's very, very long, a really difficult space, but my plan works.'

Blatt added a courtyard. 'The relocated kitchen-now-studio received a new porch, facing the new kitchen's porch and an existing porch on the guest bunkhouse. All these create a social courtyard of singular charm.'

This is just as well, because the couple seem to spend a great deal of time entertaining at this lovely old house. 'All the children and grandchildren come

when they can, and we can put them up easily. If there are too many of them to fit into the house, then they put up tents in the woods and on the lakeside. We've never run out of space.

'There's an outhouse in the field and another small house on the property, which means we can sleep quite a few families. We can put up four families in the house quite comfortably and even fit in five.' As a result, all major family reunions take place beside the lake, which she describes as 'tranquil and beautiful'.

A preservation order stipulates that the lake should be kept as wild as it was when the Norridgewick, part of the Abenaki people, hunted around its shores. 'Our lake is very large, and when we moved here its shores were unpopulated. We first rented a cottage in an American Plan Camp, where you stay in log cabins with a fireplace but no kitchen and are given three meals a day. The fishing was good and, though we didn't fish at first, we learned to. The place was so peaceful and back-to-nature. There was the chance to garden. Then we could teach the children things that were impossible in the city – they became boatsmen, they learned to swim and practise the simple life. They could see the stars without bright city lights.'

Although there has been some development around the lake, the area is still remote and wild and, thanks to the protection laws, will remain that way. 'We have moose, bear, deer, bald eagles and peregrine falcons. The moose are a problem and under state law people can hunt them once a year by lottery. It's not difficult to kill them because they stand as still as cows.'

Moose are controlled because they cause so many road accidents. 'Even if you drive at twenty-five miles an hour, if you hit one you'll probably kill it, and, even

if you get out in one piece, the collision will destroy your car. Yet it's wonderful living in this wild country. The moose are huge, with enormous racks of antlers. They are beautiful in the summer, but in spring they look just awful because they moult.'

'Black bear were seen often years ago because there were open areas for garbage dumps. When those went, they went. Now the bear are coming back again – no one can understand why. Although they've always been hunted here, they are not really dangerous unless you

come between a cub and its mother or remove food that they are planning to eat. Then they can even come into your house if they get hungry.'

So the wilderness out in Maine is quite real, and beyond the lake the high Appalachians create a rugged backdrop. The lake itself provides fish for their meals. 'The fish declined a while ago, but we asked scientists how to make it better and the fish have come back. We have landlocked salmon and rainbow trout, which we catch and grill for ourselves.'

ABOVE A bathroom with tongue-and-groove planked walls is almost totally filled by a freestanding rolltop tub.

ABOVE LEFT In keeping with the rustic character of the home, tables, chairs and table lamps on the veranda seem to be made from branches and driftwood. A collection of old hurricane lamps lines the mantelpiece.

In tune with this simple life, Paul and Mel elected to keep their home as simple as their surroundings. Stephen Blatt says, 'Our overriding challenge was to make the additions work and fit. Comfort remains the order of the day here; elegance and charm have fortuitously joined in. Various subtle touches were applied, including a bay window off the dining room, which opens the room both perceptually and in terms of function. New French doors leading from the dining room to the screen porch encourage alfresco dining.'

'It's a wonderful place for entertaining,' adds Mel. 'The main porch is big enough to fit a hundred people standing. We have buffet meals there and, although there is electricity, we use candles at night.'

Mel's and Paul's love affair with the place is by no means over. 'There are so few people here and we can't even see our neighbour's house. It's truly idyllic, a make-believe place. The world isn't this way any more. We feel extremely grateful and privileged to be here and we thank whoever made it happen every day.'

ABOVE Every wall, floor and ceiling in this bedroom is covered in tongue-and-groove planks from the local forests, all left natural, while the sharply angled ceiling is reminiscent of a roof ready to shed inches of snow. The barley-twist wooden bed, country chair, plain woollen blanket and rag rug would all appear equally at home in a pioneer's cabin.

childhood summers revisited

Traditional summer camps were set in real country with real flora and fauna. Children were treated like scouts and guides, taught how to tie knots, cook over a camp fire and wash in a bucket of cold water.

Summer camp occupies a powerful place in the collective memory of North America. Although it may have been a lot less appealing at the time, with hindsight summer camp recalls a time when the woods smelled of pine needles, when moose and bear just might be around the next tree trunk, and when meals of red flannel hash and burgers, cooked over smoking hickory wood, were the most delicious foods in the world.

How else can one explain the regular mass exodus of sophisticated urbanites to the true wilderness? Why else would those chic folk, who daily wear shined black brogues or kitten-heeled patent leathers, be willing to trade in the comfort of central heating, a myriad smart restaurants, cinema and theatre, in return for log cabins and rustic furniture that can eat opaque tights as easily as a shark gnaws a leg?

Among those attracted by the simpler rural life are Alexandra Champalimaud, an interior designer, and her businessman husband Bruce, who can leave the centre of New York and within a couple of hours cross the divide between one of the most urban landscapes on earth and rural Connecticut, where the silence is overwhelming and nature is totally in control. There are few other Western countries where such a contrast can be found in such a short space of time.

In Britain there is no wilderness to speak of – and two hours' driving from central London will take you no farther than the well-populated counties of Suffolk or Sussex. Drive a couple of hours from Paris or Rome and you will still be among agricultural fields, charming villages and advertisement hoardings. You will be fortunate to see a wild bird or any animal more unusual than a fallow deer or a fox. But travel the same distance from a big city in the USA and you are deep in forests that are as nearly untouched as when the Native American tribes hunted bear and made their canoes from the bark of the forest birch trees.

After the Native Americans, emigrants from Europe began to carve out their territories in these forests. They would built log cabins using the straight trunks of the trees they had cleared to hack out the first

ABOVE One of the many pleasures offered by the old camp is the choice of hidden corners that can be adapted for alfresco meals –such as this rustic gazebo, which overlooks the lapping waters of the lake.

OPPOSITE Whether you enjoy a spot of fishing or a gentle swing in a hammock or rocking chair, there are lots of places to relax by the lake – indoors and out. Even indoors, signs of the natural world are much in evidence, such as curved branches used for decoration. The kitchen ceiling is hung with dozens of striped paper lanterns that sway in the wind.

vegetable beds; they might introduce a few cows, pigs or hens to provide food – and, of course, they would fish in the deep lakes for the abundant freshwater varieties of shellfish and trout. Nowadays it is possible to have the enjoyment of the wilderness – the brilliant stars undimmed by city lights, the silence of the forests broken by the eerie cries of nature's hunters and hunted, the soft lapping of the water – with the added bonus of central heating, air conditioning in summer, effective screens against mosquitoes, and a four-wheel-drive car to make short work of the trip from Manhattan to Connecticut.

Camp Kent, 30 years ago, was a place for children set beside the shores of a typically forested lake in the north of the country. In its heyday it had consisted of a large group of clapboard buildings clustered around the shores; these were intended as dormitories and recreational buildings for the children who arrived every summer. But such camps were going out of favour with the American public who, instead, were becoming avid for a piece of wild nature all their own.

Planning laws and controls over new building, altering the wilderness or creating the infrastructure people need today were becoming increasingly strict, to the extent that it was quite often impossible to develop new collections of buildings in particularly lovely areas. One solution was to find run-down houses, put up in a less strict era, and transform them into weekend homes for today.

Alexandra Champalimaud's husband found Camp Kent when it was declining and the owner was open to the idea of selling. 'While local zoning laws theoretically allowed several hundred condominiums to be built on the property, the owner was only prepared to sell to someone who would change the property minimally. My future husband and a couple of friends could not resist this little corner of Connecticut, lost down a dirt road, but less than two hours from Manhattan.'

The buildings were in a bad state, having had three decades of fierce storms and icy winters to weather, but the position was superb. 'The crumbling camp buildings were removed, except for the five that had life in them. A compound was made around a big barn overhanging the lake, which had been the Camp Kent theatre. This theatre is now the soul of our retreat.'

The main house has eight bedrooms. There are also a guesthouse with two bedrooms and an Adirondack-style cabin, which can fit in another seven guests. The whole is set in 6 hectares of wilderness. It is not unknown for up to 24 colleagues, friends and family to meet here for a weekend. Alexandra loves entertaining – when she's not revamping the Algonquin hotel, decorating a couple of houses in Aspen or building another home in New Mexico. 'I can organize food for twenty in two minutes,' she says. 'I grew up in a house that was constantly full, so I got used to it.'

Creating the whole holiday home, however, was not so instant. 'Before the camp became a home, we spent

THIS PAGE The pioneering bit – playing for a while at being a fur trapper for the Hudson's Bay Company, a Native American scout, a fisherman making his own canoe out of birch bark, or a farmer ready to clear and burn his own patch for growing corn – digs deep into the American psyche.

OPPOSITE Rough twigs from the surrounding forests, along with logs and bleached decking, create a gazebo attached to the house and at the far end of the veranda.

hours prospecting and redesigning, trying to make sense of the rustic camp bunks, the music room, the old infirmary and the nearly collapsed theatre. While I tried to add my energy and "edge" to my new friends' vision, our children forged their friendships through theatricals and productions of their own in the theatre.'

Alexandra has been careful not to lose any of the charm of this ancient group of buildings hidden down a track. 'The style, if you can call it that, is simplified Adirondack, with a branch – bark and all – holding the shower curtain, for example. I chose to change the red and white vernacular to dark red with brown/black trim because we learned that the natural and dark colours "disappeared" into the woods around – even in the leafless Connecticut winter.'

Most rooms are timber clad with the planks arranged horizontally, as in all the best log cabins. Indeed, they are cubes of timber with planked and beamed ceilings, and floors of yet more planks. None is painted. The furniture also appears basic. The chairs look as though they were made by a pioneer working with bare branches, while pictures are propped on shelves more often than hung. Colours everywhere are soft and subtle – whites, creams, off-whites, bleached woods, a touch of Swedish

TOP The main bedroom has been arranged and decorated with great simplicity.

ABOVE Imaginative use of decking is in evidence throughout the property.

LEFT Curved branches, found in the nearby woods, give the impression of holding up the rough stone fireplace – although, of course, in reality they don't.

FAR LEFT Alexandra was far too clever to cover over the graffiti created by earlier visitors to the camp, who painted and scrawled their names all over the kitchen wall and doors. They add greatly to the atmosphere.

THIS PAGE AND OPPOSITE, BELOW The floor, walls and ceiling in the living room are made of natural wood, and some of the furniture has survived from the time when the place was a camp. One end of the living room leads to the main bedroom, while the other opens onto a veranda.

OPPOSITE, ABOVE LEFT A whole array of waders and skating boots, rubber boots and anti-mosquito hats are lined up in the hallway.

OPPOSITE, ABOVE RIGHT A guest bedroom's walls reach only to the rafters, leaving empty space above for ventilation and inter-room conversations.

green on a painted table. The spirit of long-departed holiday children lives on in names daubed on the walls. 'If Camp Kent has a single memorable detail,' says Alexandra, 'it's the names of generations of campers scrawled in paint that remain in the kitchen – plus the names of our family and friends who have worked on weekends to help us bring the theatre back to life. As our families fell in love with each other, this little lake filled with drinking-quality water became more than a swimming and fishing dock to us.' It became a place that held the soul of their family.

Their intense involvement in its magic and its purity made the family determined to preserve this remote corner of Connecticut. 'It retains that summer-camp feeling that brings a smile to every face. The theatre is the ultimate party barn in the summer and a broom-hockey or ping-pong room on those frigid winter days.

'Camp Kent remains a camp for all ages of the family and our friends which is shared with abundant wild life – beaver, otters, wild turkey, deer, eagles, hawks, ruffled grouse and the occasional black bear or coyote – along with all the little creatures of the New England woods. The lake is full of bass and pike, along with freshwater prawns and mussels. There is a great trout stream only ten minutes away.'

One of their neighbours is a professional hydrologist who has made it his business to ensure that the purity of the water – which can be drunk directly from the lake – is never lost.

'He patrols daily in his wetsuit,' explains Alexandra. 'Whenever I pass him in my kayak he can provide a report on his latest measurement of water purity. We allow no motors on the lake, and take every precaution that his measurements never signal damage from the presence of the community. The local ice fishermen help preserve the area too, and their little shacks represent an enjoyable alternative to a local pub at the end of a winter walk.'

At the back of the lake are forests. 'The woodlands, wetlands and meadows give us all the pleasures of the four full seasons in the New England woods. While the fall colours are world-famous, and early spring is a study in delicacy, most spectacular is the June explosion of pink mountain laurel on the ledges of the hillsides that run down to the lake – except perhaps when the icy winter arrives quickly on a windless day, freezing the lake into a clear sheet of glass through which you can see to the bottom of the lake. Last year we enjoyed a spectacular, sunny afternoon skating across the top of this crystal aquarium.'

fire and ice in Maine

It would be hard to guess that this characterful house replaces an earlier version that literally blew up after a lightning strike within a short while of the new owner moving in.

Lynn, a photographer, knows all about the problems of owning a house on a remote lake shore. The first accident that happened to her old cottage in Maine was, it is true, only tenuously connected with water, in that storms and gales often seem to be worse near water. One June day in 1992 – when, luckily, she was away – the trees around her house were struck by lightning. 'I'm told that the trees were struck and the house literally blew up,' she says. 'It was the force of the electricity that went through the tree roots and under the house, which was on stilts against flooding. The whole thing just ignited. It was totally demolished.'

Eight years later, and after a prolonged pause for thought, she admits that, now, she's glad it happened. 'The fact that it burned down changed a lot for me. Without that, I might not have moved here. It was

THIS PAGE AND
OPPOSITE After the fire,
Lynn was allowed to rebuild
on the same 'footprint' and
decided that everything
should look as if it had been
there for ever. Wooden
shingles cover the outside
veranda walls, with other
woodwork painted Shaker
blue – the same colour as the
Adirondack chairs set on
plain bleached-wood floors.

actually worse, in a way, to lose the trees.' The fire
gave Lynn the chance to rebuild on the same site, just
2 metres from the water's edge. If it had not occurred,
she would have been allowed neither to extend the
tiny cottage nor to pull it down and rebuild. But the
state authorities agreed that she could create another
house, provided that it was on the same 'footprint' as
the old house's frontage. At the back she was given
more leeway and allowed to build upwards. Her chosen
architect was Stephen Blatt, and her instructions were
clear: she wanted the new house 'to look as though it
had always been there'.

The result was so successful that the cottage won
Blatt an Honor Award from the Maine Chapter of the
American Institute of Architects in 1995 and, in 2000,
another from the New England Design Awards. 'We
were commissioned to replace the cottage, not with

a replica but with a year-round home providing the
equivalent amount of peace, quiet and memories,' says
Stephen Blatt. 'Land-use regulation allowed rebuilding
on the old footprint with conditions: no more than
25 per cent expansion, 30 per cent volume expansion.

'The original one-storey structure contained minimal
volume under a simple roof. To abide by the footprint
limitation, bedrooms are on an upper level. Under
the gables, porches surround the house; their depth,
especially at the corners, is enunciated by the shallow
pitch of the perimeter roofs. Windows are small and
simple and the detailing is straightforward and rugged.

'The house, approached from deep woods, beckons
with broad sitting steps leading up to a sheltered
porch and a screened dining porch. Upstairs a guest
room faces north, while the owner's bedroom suite
has water views in three directions.'

THIS PAGE AND OPPOSITE Who could resist placing a carved wooden swan by the living-room windows that overlook the waters of the lake? Here, as in the rest of the house, colours are subordinated to the views. Upholstery is neutral, and everywhere there are comfortable old chairs cushioned in well-washed fabrics. Lynn's black labrador is called BJ and his favourite days are spent on the shores of the lake, where he can gambol and swim.

The attractions of the place include the constant changes wrought by the water and the wildlife it attracts. There are bass, perch, salmon and trout in the lake, and colourful water birds. 'The loons are the main birds here. They're large and not good on land, so they mostly need to paddle. They nest by the shore, but we do our best to leave them alone. They are wonderful to look at – black with white accent feathers.'

Migrating bufflehead ducks and hooded mergansers come in their hundreds and may stay for only a day. An otter lives on the property. There are wild turkeys, and beavers arrived two years ago. The beavers cut down one of the poplar trees but so far the wonderful pines, hemlocks and cedar evergreens, along with the oaks, maples, beeches and birches that cluster on the point, have survived intact.

BELOW The morning light streams in through the bathroom window, whose windows are shaded by translucent white curtains. Tongue-and-groove planking painted in watery colours is the order of the day for the walls and cupboards.

'The lake freezes in winter and the ice is sometimes covered in snow – so we do a lot of skating or skiing. My black labrador loves to run around on the ice. Then ice fishermen come and put up shacks all around us.'

The weather is another prominent feature. 'It can be very windy and stormy but also quite magnificent,' says Lynn. 'One phenomenon that happens in April is that the ice breaks up in the lake and flows with the current to one end. A couple of years ago the wind changed as this was happening and started pushing the ice to the north, up to my house. The ice piled up all around the shore and I was afraid it was going to come up onto the porch. It was extraordinary – in little pieces like ice cubes, piling up towards me and tinkling as they rolled over . . . bizarre and scary.'

When the ice is intact, however, and as long as the snow hasn't fallen, she can skate along the lake as far as the local town, which is reached by sailing boat in summer. 'My boat is easy to sail because it is so small. I've also taken a fishing boat with a motor to the town and paddled a canoe there. There's a little place where we can eat, so we go there in summer.'

Since the terrible day of the lightning strike the trees and underbrush have grown back, and the house is settling down to look even more mature and established. Perhaps it was a lucky strike after all.

THIS PAGE AND OPPOSITE, ABOVE The bed in Lynn's room (opposite) is covered with a favourite blanket – a gift from her mother – and a newer one by Ralph Lauren, while the tiny guest room (this page) has a fine log-cabin quilt on the bed.

riverside living

From thundering torrent to placid flow, from mountain stream to lazy estuary, all riverside locations have one thing in common: a sense of the water's journey from source to sea – but, beyond that, riverside living offers amazing variety.

a work of art in wood

Overlooking a tidal creek in south-west England, amid lusciously green valleys, is a timber-framed house that was rebuilt using traditional crafts dating back more than 700 years.

Everyone in the know about house-buying says that the secret is location, location, location, since the panorama, the silence of the countryside or the soft murmur of the sea is the one part of a house that cannot be changed. The wisdom of this view is exemplifed by Seagull House. This was once a plain house with little to distinguish it – but that was before 1988, when Roderick James and his wife Gillie moved in with their three sons. They had come from Gloucestershire to the far West Country – a long way, in English terms – for a single,

ABOVE The main living space recalls the inside of an upturned hull. The entire room serves as a reminder of Roderick James's love affair with timber – as does the Seagull House sign.

TOP LEFT The glass walls of the dining room would, in medieval times, have been filled with wattle and daub. In the 21st century, glass gives far more light and accentuates the views.

LEFT The clapboard exterior of Gillie's studio is painted a muted American red.

OPPOSITE Verandas were built all around the original building to create a series of sheltered, semi-outdoor rooms at ground level, while on the upper level each bedroom gained an outdoor platform to allow occupants to enjoy the beautiful views.

simple reason: the house's position. It stands above a tidal creek in Devon amid green wooded valleys that climb steeply up from the water.

Roderick is an architect who has been in practice since 1974 working with oak barns. He is also in partnership with a friend, Charles Brentnall, in the firm Carpenter Oak and Woodland, which creates new timber-framed buildings using traditional crafts with a contemporary spin. Roderick had become concerned

ABOVE Gillie's studio walls are ornamented with lively examples of her work.

ABOVE RIGHT The muted colours and designs that characterize the interior of the house itself are offset by bright fabrics, casually slung.

RIGHT The James family may have up to ten boats on the creek at any time, for sailing or enjoying a relaxing session on the water.

OPPOSITE One of the first things that Roderick did to his dull building was to give it ground-floor verandas and upper-floor balconies. Among the examples of American East Coast style are the welcoming Adirondack chairs on the decking.

'Everyone loves living by the water; people are drawn to it because it is fundamental to life. Once you come to live by the water, you'll never go away.'

about the spate of barn conversions in which great and ancient spaces across the country were clumsily carved up into family homes. Careless conversion, he felt, resulted in 'the loss of drama and space'. Yet he understood the demand for dramatic open-plan rural homes, and wanted to offer the same theatricality in houses constructed from scratch for a modern way of life. The firm now has four separate yards, from Devon to Scotland, and employs 60 carpenters.

Seagull House, designed and built by Roderick James with both his hats on, is rather more traditional than his current work. It serves as not only a family home but also a place to talk to clients and demonstrate

Although the James family's creekside home is very much a working establishment, it is also a treasure trove of maritime equipment, such as old ropes and lifebelts. In the well-used mud room, brilliantly coloured windcheaters, wellington boots and swimming flippers mingle with old model yachts, rows of hurricane lanterns and locally found animals' skulls and agricultural implements.

what can be done with wood and building techniques that have been practised in England and Wales for more than seven centuries.

The house is very different from the 1950s block that the James family took on. It now consists of the original building 'bungalow-eaten' with wooden cladding, clinker-built for a fine nautical effect and enlivened by a ground-level veranda and a first-floor balcony. Then there is a new, full-scale timber-framed 'barn' using trusses, beams and joints developed in England before 1300, and between the two is a single-storey link that accommodates Gillie James's studio.

Gillie works there on semi-figurative oil paintings and makes the colourful traditional patchwork quilts which she sells and which appear throughout the house. This building is also covered with wooden cladding and, like the other two, roofed in slate. The three enclose a courtyard garden, planted with ebullient greenery. The entire complex fits snugly into the surrounding woods. The result is a rambling, complicated building with, Roderick says, enormous variety in its spaces and angles. None of the rooms

rivals in drama the great expanse of the barn, which is not divided into rooms except for a gallery. Vast braced collar trusses stabilize the whole area, whose purpose is to show off the skilled carpentry of his firm. There is neither a ceiling nor any attempt to conceal the beams and braces.

The floor is pale wood, as is much of the furniture, while sofas and chairs are covered in plain colours. Natural light pours down from roof lights, and a huge log fire is of near-brutalist concrete with faux tiles painted on by Gillie. Decoy birds and Gillie's paintings are the only decoration.

The couple used to make decoys for a living, and made several trips to the East Coast of the USA, where the wooden water birds are so imaginatively carved. The influence of the maritime East Coast states – whether in the construction of Seagull House, its colouring or the use of light – is evident throughout.

A scale model of a typical timber frame stands on a table beside the building's front door in an area which acts as both an office and reception area for clients and the dining area of the barn. Its timbered walls are

ABOVE One of the spare
bedrooms has this nautically
themed bathroom en suite.
The walls are constructed
of very rough sawn boards,
with marine caulk used in
between. Being in the
bathroom feels similar to
being in an old wooden ship.

infilled not with wattle and daub but with great slabs
of glass which give enormous sweeping views across
the garden to the quiet creek beyond.

Of course, the whole point of the complex design is
to emphasize these views over the water and woods.
This is why the wide, balustraded balcony provides
wide vistas from the bedrooms of visitors and the
family alike. Nearly 2.5 metres above the ground, it
runs around the entire area of the original house and
every bedroom opens onto it. People can walk all
around it, taking in the generous southern English
scenery. The rooms' French windows are glazed and
painted a soft sea blue, and there are comfortable
wooden American chairs for lounging during open-air
summer breakfasts and siestas. In winter the same
walkway offers the chance to spot migrant shorebirds
arriving from the sea. Similar chairs turn up in the
garden and on the veranda under the balustrade, which
is, of course, protected from the rain.

At Seagull House and in the waterside homes he
designs for clients, Roderick James is always conscious
of the location, be it by the sea, an estuary or a river.

He likes to give each its own sophisticated nautical
feeling, alluding to the rigging of boats, to jetties
and balconies. Everywhere he tries to maximize the
peculiar light, shadows and ripple effect that come
from moving water. He calls it 'glintering'. 'It's
important to get the angles and positions right for
the sun, the water and the roofs to ensure that light
bounced off the water reflects on the ceilings.'

In Seagull House you will discover model yachts in
bathrooms and bedrooms and given prime position at
the end of the dining room. There are decoy birds
everywhere, too – wild ducks, geese, and shorebirds
such as snipe and sandling. The Jameses even made
their own metal cut-out curlew stick-up decoys which
are driven into the mud of the creek with integral
poles. 'We know they work because the day after we
set up 13 of them, each had a seagull on its head!'

The way the wood is used inside also recalls
maritime buildings and ships' cabins. Bedrooms and
bathrooms are panelled with planks which, unusually,
run horizontally rather than in vertical lines. The
planks are roughly sawn and the joints filled with

a marine caulk of soft white. By contrast, Gillie's studio is painted white throughout – floor, walls, ceiling – allowing the strong colours of her paintings and quilts to provide the interest.

Roderick is extremely proud of his nautical blood, which may explain why he feels so at home working with wood and water. 'My forebears were sea captains, the owners of barques, schooners, brigantines. I have a genetic link with the sea, and I have always had boats.' He has them still – no fewer than six can be

seen from Seagull House, moored across the creek. The house's mud room is filled with the primary shades of oilskins and slickers, sea boots and flippers, jammed in with more model yachts and hurricane lanterns.

There are dozens of lanterns, which are brought out to welcome and illuminate the way to Seagull House for party guests on dark nights. It is a practice utterly in keeping with the waterside setting, where lights have been used for centuries to guide and cheer travellers, fishermen and sailors.

ABOVE AND OPPOSITE, RIGHT A 19th-century family portrait turned out to be exactly the right size to fit, floor to ceiling, in this guest bedroom. The iron bed, painted white, is covered in one of Gillie's pretty quilts, whose sandy colours with splashes of blue pick up the muted decorative theme of the rest of the room. The walls recall a log cabin.

a boat-lover's paradise

Rowing, sailing and fishing are the favourite pastimes on this secluded Australian island, which remains largely native bush.

The architect Terry Dorrough lives on Dangar Island on the Hawkesbury river near Sydney. Until the mid-19th century, the island was occupied by Australian aboriginal people, as evidenced by the rock art and shell middens scattered around the place. But in the 1780s, says Terry, 'The governor of Australia came with his crew to explore the river and camped on the island, calling it Mullet Island. In 1864 the island was bought from the Crown by the Dangar family, who in the 1880s built a large holiday home there as a retreat from their home in Sydney. The Dangar house was used as a guest house until it burned down in 1939. Very little of the original now remains, apart from a stone tower and an old

boatshed.' What the Dangars were doing in the 1880s, other Sydney folk were doing in the 1980s, so today there are about 200 homes on the island, owned either by people who live there full-time or by those who live and work in Sydney but travel across to the island by boat for relaxed weekends.

'We lived for a year in the small boatshed/cottage on the waterfront while planning the new house. This gave us time to experience the site in different seasons and at different times of the day and night,' explains Terry, who runs his architectural practice from home. 'I had become involved in a community-funded management plan for the island, aimed at preserving its unique character, and helped to persuade the local

THIS PAGE AND
OPPOSITE The secret of
Terry Dorrough's success has
been to make the interior
and the exterior of the house
interchangeable. Verandas
and decking are used to
bring the sunshine and views
into the rooms, while more
decking and corrugated-iron
roofs link the various parts of
the building, which has been
constructed on three levels.
The house was carefully
positioned to take advantage
of the trees and shrubs on
the slopes, and its yellow
walls are perfectly coloured
to catch leafy shadows.

Hornsby Council to adopt a strong development-
control plan. Our aim was to fit into the context of
timber-and-fibro weekenders, boatsheds and jetties.
We were not interested in fashion or style but in a
house that really worked as a place to live.'

The new house steps up the slope on three levels,
carefully sited to preserve existing trees and maximize
access to sunlight and views. Its main living area has
a strong post-and-beam timber frame, which contrasts
with the coloured aluminium sliding and pivoting
doors. The doors can be thrown open for most of the
year to transform the living area, kitchen and veranda
into one high, flowing space. Beyond the stone
fireplace, the bedroom and shower room open onto a
screened porch, which invites in filtered morning sun
and evening moonlight.

The colours – muted warm greys, yellows and off-
whites, and cooler purple greys – were inspired by
the seasonal changes in the trunks of the surrounding
Blackbutt trees. 'Seen from the river, the wide gable

of the veranda/living area echoes, on a larger scale,
the existing cottage/boatshed,' says Terry. 'The north-
facing waterfront site, sheltered from southerlies and
winter westerlies, has a fairly ideal microclimate.'

The house is flooded with sun in winter, thanks to
the high gable roof, north-facing glazing and ridge
skylight. The open fire gives enough heating for the
living area, and its central location helps to warm the
bedroom. For Terry Dorrough, the house is a spacious,
workable and stimulating living environment, built on
a difficult site for a very modest cost.

Costing cannot have been easy, for Dangar Island is,
like Venice, surrounded by sea and not suited to cars.
There is no access to the island for the transport of
materials except by barge. The roads, though formed,
are essentially for pedestrian and wheelbarrow traffic.
Translate that into the fact that every single necessity
for the new house arrived by barge and was taken to
the site thereafter by wheelbarrow. 'We acted as
owner-builders in order to keep control of costs and

allow for experiment and change as the work went on,' says Terry. 'We were fortunate to have skilled local carpenters who built the house to a "lock-up" stage while we, over time, completed the finishes, built-in joinery and so on.'

The house was planned around a series of outdoor sitting, dining and working spaces, to take advantage of different aspects of the site and for use in different seasons or at different times of day.

On the principal axis from the water, a waterfront working deck extends out from the boatshed, and a roof deck – a place to relax near the water – has been built over the boatshed. On the main level is a large covered outdoor room for year-round living, while the courtyard deck on the middle level is a sheltered sun trap. The grass terrace above the house is tree-shaded and cool in summer, and immediately below the house is a moon-viewing terrace with barbecue. On the cross axis there is an additional western deck to let winter sun flow into the dining area, and an eastern screen porch for filtered morning sun and evening moonlight to shine into the bedroom and shower.

A lot of the island is still native bush, and the 200-odd home owners are determined to keep it that way.

Since the island is quite small there are no large animals such as kangaroo, but there is an abundance of birds, some of them quite demanding. 'Kookaburras, magpies, currawongs and rainbow lorikeets regularly land on the veranda rail, demanding in raucous voices to be fed. The lorikeets screech like small parrots and are very colourful. Possums clamber over the roof and make quite a noise, too.'

A major pleasure for everyone is boating. 'Boating and fishing are, of course, common pastimes on the island,' says Terry Dorrough. 'The majority of people have a "tinny" – an aluminium boat with outboard motor that is used for commuting. Rowing is popular, too. There is an annual round-the-island rowing race at Easter. I also have a small yacht and sail regularly in the nearby waterways.'

Like everyone who lives beside the water, Terry is captivated by the constant change it offers. 'It's rather similar to living in the mountains. You get a wider view of the world around you. Somehow, nature is always there but different every day. We are tidal, so the river is never static, and at night there's the moon or stars shining on the water.

'I think being by the water exaggerates everything. When it's calm, it's very calm, and when there are storms you get the worst of it. You are very aware of the weather – unlike living in the bush or the suburbs. We are well attuned to the island because we have to deal with it every day. We come and go, using the boat, at high and low tide. Sydney is only ten minutes away in the boat, then a train journey of an hour into the centre. But you can come back at night when the weather is filthy, nasty.'

Terry owns a small fleet of water craft: 'My boats include a runabout with an outboard, a small sailing boat and a racing yacht. Mostly we take the yacht for a day's sailing but we can spend a night away on it. There are so many places to sail, intricate ins and outs. We don't have to go to the ocean. All around here is national park, protected.

'I have been sailing since I was a boy and have always loved the water and boats. I introduced my wife to sailing when we were first married and, although she is not madly keen, she accepts a boat-orientated life.' I know the feeling exactly.

australian dream time

Tranquillity and solitude are the main features
of life on the banks of this drowned valley.

There's waterside living and there's living on an island, which is something entirely different. A house at the waterside is at a dead end. Instead of a circumference of places to go from home, you have only 180° worth, unless you are intrepid enough to take to the water in a boat. Living on an island is a choice in isolation. You are not necessarily cut off from the rest of the world, but you are very much part of a chosen community. Island dwellers can feel as though they are living in a remote mountain village. You know everyone and everyone knows you; the only way to enjoy life is to make sure that you fit in. If you don't, woe betide you.

Dangar Island in Australia features twice in this book (Terry Dorrough's home is on pages 60–65) because it obviously attracts people who are looking for that quality of remoteness and isolation found on islands and yet, at the same time, for surroundings which can be quickly changed – for the city of Sydney is just around the corner.

Les Reedman, who is both a chartered architect and an architectural historian, managed to combine the life of an islander with a busy architectural practice in Sydney itself. 'My house was my weekend retreat from the city. It's on an island near the outlet of a broad east-coast river, the Hawkesbury. The island's beach, which the house overlooks, was visited by officers of the British First Fleet within weeks of their arrival in 1788 at Port Jackson farther south.'

The house is now his full-time home and Sydney is visited only from time to time. 'My house is a modest two-bedroom "cabin" with a full-width veranda facing east across the river to the sandstone cliffs. It is built of lightweight timber framing clad mainly with glass in timber frames. This is a practical construction for a dwelling across a waterway in a temperate climate; what's more, most rooms get a view.'

Les's drawings for the house show at least six areas for beds, and other parts are identified by words such as 'Dream', 'Write', 'Relax', 'Potter' and 'Cook', while at the edge of the building are designated water views, fishing and swimming areas, and steep steps that lead to the forest at the back of the house. 'When I bought the property in 1970 it had a dilapidated fibro-clad fisherman's shack built after World War Two from this

THIS PAGE A major change carried out by Les was to install a wide veranda, which takes full advantage of the view and the shipping lanes beyond. Inside the house he has added occasional touches such as a deep-brimmed hat (to guard against insects) and a book on how to tell what has stung you.

OPPOSITE Fishermen don't have everything easy. Greedy representatives of the local birdlife such as pelicans can get there first.

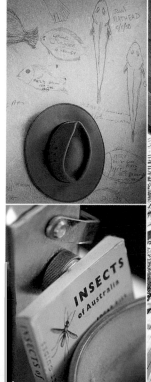

and that. It had two small rooms and a minuscule veranda with lots of fish drawings on the wall – the work of the previous occupants. I kept the core rooms and built a surrounding lightweight structure, which provides a generous veranda and bathroom, sleepout, laundry and kitchen – all with views.'

The Hawkesbury river is wide and interesting, with wooded banks interspersed with cliffs rolling up at each side. 'The veranda has extensive views over the river to the sandstone cliffs, which glow in the afternoon sun. There are hundreds of Aboriginal rock carvings on the hills all round the river, evidence of an earlier habitation.'

So, while the area appears to have a history which dates back to the 1780s and the first white settlers, in fact it spirals back into prehistory. 'The estuary is a drowned valley after the rise of the sea tens of thousands of years ago. The river catchment is very extensive, draining a high rainfall from as far south as inland Goulburn and up to the Great Dividing Coastal Range in the west. The river has worn its way in time through sandstone, which has resulted in many figured cliffs and sculptured rock outcrops, hundreds of feet

ABOVE AND BELOW The trick with an unassuming house such as this old fisherman's shack is to allow all the details to blend in. Les has made little attempt to find grand or over-stylish furniture, using his eye instead to find pieces from the mid-20th century.

OPPOSITE One of the most interesting features of the original shack was that the previous occupants – all fishermen – had sketched the varieties and sizes of the local fish on the building's wall – and I bet they used a bit of fishermen's licence.

The estuary is both wild and tidal – though not as fierce at the ocean beyond. Islanders such as Les Reedman are constantly exploring its channels, fishing like the owners of the original cabin, and enjoying the full scope of island life.

high, from the Blue Mountains to the sea. 'There is much evidence that the Dharug Aboriginal tribe lived in the area before white settlement. There are many shell middens on salient points around the river, and there are the rock carvings on elevated flat-rock areas which command water views important in their ceremonies. The carvings show the outlines mainly of fish, snakes and wallabies – wildlife that can be still seen today, but which has been much diminished by encroaching development.'

The modern primitive drawings of fish that Les Reedman has so cleverly kept on the walls of his

converted home make a parallel with these ancient carvings, and, he says, the birdlife around is still plentiful and similar to what the Aboriginal people would have known – kookaburras, sea eagles, whistling kites and pelicans, all birds of the sea.

'The first houses on the island were constructed for workers of the Brooklyn Bridge Company, which built the nearby main Northern Rail Bridge across the Hawkesbury in the 1880s, completing the rail link from Sydney to the north. The bridge was opened in 1889 by Sir Henry Parker, the New South Wales premier, who noted that it was a first step to the Federation of Australian states. Ten years later the drafting party of the Federation spent a weekend on a steamboat here, no doubt to conclude the constitution.'

Some time in the 1920s living on Dangar Island became desirable. 'The island was subdivided for house lots then and the first river dwellings began to appear. Today there are almost 200 houses, a bowling club, community hall, fire station and shop.'

A ferry service connects the island and river with the mainland Brooklyn township. Rather than rely on the ferry, most inhabitants are happy to sail across from the island to the mainland and then continue by train to Sydney. 'I have a boatshed and a couple of boats,' says Reedman, 'one to cross the channel to the mainland and the other, a bit bigger, to sail around the estuary. I go fishing when I can.'

The estuary is both wild and tidal though not, of course, as fierce at the real ocean beyond. Islanders such as Reedman are constantly exploring its channels, fishing like the owners of the original cabin, and enjoying the full scope of island life. To that end the rooms of the house are simple and relaxed. The floors

are of wood, with the wooden frames of the windows also left natural. Feathers are propped against seascapes and, outside, gum trees lean over almost into the veranda and the huge windows.

The whole building seems as if it is constructed of glass, and if you are fortunate enough to sail by on the river below at dusk, as the lights come on you will catch a glimpse of this impressive building, in character like a giant boathouse or barn with its low-pitched roof shining out against the silhouettes of the trees all around.

Despite the pressures for residential and commercial development in this area, Reedman can still call Dangar Island 'a pristine environment'. The reason is that the residents are 'extremely protective' of their beautiful island – which, he says, 'remains heavily timbered with large native eucalyptus, wattles and native flowering shrubs.'

The trouble with writing this book is that, with every case study I write, I wish I was there for ever.

THIS PAGE AND OPPOSITE All around the converted fisherman's shack are places to sit for meals, for relaxation and for river viewing. The majority of the inhabitants of Dangar Island have boats – not simply for hobby sailing, but to travel to meet friends and even to go to work in nearby Sydney.

going Dutch in Paris

This is the story of a snapper-up of unconsidered trifles, a great rummager in flea markets, antique shops and even skips – so it is hardly surprising that his boat was bought by accident too.

Having decided that a boat would make a much better value home than a house or apartment in London, Rupert Morgan went to a boatyard with something small and cheap in mind – and ended up with a 23-metre-long Tjaalk built in 1913. 'The Dutch built boats like these for 400 years, up to the First World War,' he explains. 'Mine is one of the last, with steel planks used in exactly the same way as wooden planks were in earlier versions. It is 4.3 metres wide and weighs 50 tonnes.'

When Rupert saw the boat, 'There was sunlight pouring in from every direction, teak parquet flooring, a big living room, three bedrooms and two bathrooms. It had central heating and a wood-burning stove, plus a choice of three forms of electricity: mains, battery or the biggest generator you've ever seen. It had a two-tiered deck, with room for a dining table, deckchairs, a herb garden and an inflatable swimming pool. The only problem was that it might, in rare circumstances, sink.' It was love at first sight.

'Travelling in your own boat causes zero stress. You are not wrecking the countryside. It is just that the unspoiled places cannot be reached by car. I know hundreds of idyllic spots, some of them just outside towns, where nothing has changed in a hundred years. But you can only get there by water.'

Rupert is adept at carpentry. 'Most things on a boat need to be built-in because the walls are not straight, but we have tried to make everything look as though it was always there.' What was already there was the wheelhouse with steps leading to a two-level saloon with a curved wooden sofa. The bathroom and shower were also there in 1913, but the Morgans made the tiny kitchen. 'It's like a cockpit. Everything is within reach, and we can make really good meals in there.'

There is a downside. 'The things we take for granted on dry land are operated by machines: drinking-water pump, waste-water pump, electric lavatories. They can go wrong.' Indeed, they go wrong so often that the Morgans are expert at fixing them. 'It's nasty work – for some reason it always involves sticking your head into some rank-smelling greasy recess with a torch in your mouth.' But it makes no difference to their love of the boat. Even trips to London are heavenly. 'When you're on the river, London is a beautiful town, with clean air and magnificent sunsets.'

THIS PAGE AND OPPOSITE Karin is responsible for the choice of fabrics such as the jolly shower curtain. The walls behind the bath are papered with advertisements from a 1920s lifestyle magazine, while the mirror belonged to Karin's grandparents. Karin also took some excerpts from Rupert's unpublished novel to print on the duvet cover. The brass lamps that are seen everywhere on the boat are old stage footlights.

Bachelor Rupert set sail along canals and rivers and, in extremely calm weather, across stretches of sea. He also gave up his day job in advertising for a novelist's life, and has since published two satires, *Let There Be Life* and *Something Sacred*. Then he married Karin and they now have two young daughters.

Rupert becomes lyrical when talking about the boat. 'There is something about living on a boat that is not normal life. One enters an entirely different world. We're moored in the middle of Paris but there are ducks, swans and turtles swimming past.

'The reason I bought the boat was simply economic – it was all I could afford – but, apart from those people who get discouraged, everyone who tries it catches the bug. Boating is like luxury camping: you're aware of the weather, you hear the rain falling – there's a great feeling of liberty. It's wonderful to pull up anchor and take your home with you.

LEFT Houseboats have plenty of wide flat decks, and here they are used to full advantage for a thriving garden. Bamboos, bays and other shrubs chosen for their interesting foliage are planted in pots, so that the boat blends in with the banks of the river beyond.

RIGHT Muted wooden chairs and tables stand on bleached decking surrounded by pots of leafy shrubs. What a place for a sunny breakfast.

a very French houseboat

Its style reflects the sophisticated Parisian view of a French cottage, with few concessions made to the fact that this is a home on water.

Home for one former designer is a houseboat moored on the Seine not far from the centre of Paris. Rectangular and far from aerodynamic, the boat looks as though it was never intended to move from the banks. It is, somehow, a very French houseboat. Half is given over to a two-storey section where the less ornate rooms – a ground-floor main bedroom and bathroom, a kitchen plus two more bedrooms up a narrow stairway – are housed. The rest is half-open deck with, below it, an all-white living room where comfortable sofas and chairs face out onto the fast-flowing river below. 'My decorator and I decided to use simple, natural fabrics and decor in this area. We put in a whitened wooden floor and lots of woven willow, sisal and natural linen.'

From the sunny deck above or, on cold winter days, behind the enormous glass windows of the salon, the owner becomes part of the busy life of Paris's great river. Mallards and other wildfowl often appear on deck, and their quacking serves as an

The gnarled fishermen with their lines and berets, the river traffic of working barges, and the wildfowl that fly in to land nearby: all add to the appeal of life on the Seine.

early-morning call. 'I love it here, the nature and the ducks. It's a perfect place to live. I would never leave.' The designer first encountered the houseboat in 1989. 'It was a *coup de foudre* when I saw the boat. She was ancient and far too small. The *coque* [hull] was in a pitiable state. But one thing really pleased me: I knew that, without any motor, she would never set sail.'

She called in her friend and decorator Julie Prisca to help to repair and modernize the boat. The result is an interior that pays no attention to the boat's location other than to celebrate the marvellous views virtually at water level. Every corner has little bouquets of scented flowers, pink roses and cottagey bunches, teamed with small table lights. There are shelves full of elegant books with, above, the owner's collection of ornamental hands – iron paperweights, bits taken from artists' wooden models or from wooden statues. Julie added table sculptures of dried leaves, carefully placed among oriental bowls and small woven baskets.

The dining area also overlooks the river – a small table surrounded by ironwork chairs. The whole turns outwards, towards the busy Seine and the green banks of Paris beyond. A plain gangplank, covered in bright green, with rails handy for parking the bike, leads to the shore, which seems a million miles away.

The two women have brought a sophisticated Parisian view of a French cottage onto a houseboat. All is comfort and light, helped by the use of white throughout. The beamed ceilings are white, as is the spiral staircase which leads from inside the front door to the upstairs of the boat. Apart from the bedrooms, the walls are a matte white, as are the heavy Roman blinds and cushions in the elegant living room.

There is little sign of clutter. With each small painting, gilded hand or antique sculptured head used to maximum effect, it is no surprise to learn that the owner hopes soon to open her own *brocante* shop full of sophisticated finds.

TOP The gangway (handy for parking the bike) leads into the two-storey section with its iron spiral stairs.

LEFT The main living room in the boat's single-storey section is all white, from sofas to Roman blinds. Huge windows look out over the river, but, apart from the view, this living room could be in a Parisian apartment.

FAR LEFT Wildfowl are drawn to the houseboat in large numbers. Mallards are regular visitors, while swans slide past its bows.

clifftop living

A clifftop home is the most exciting of all waterside locations. Although lacking the romance of a beach, it has wide panoramas and big skies. Its storms can be dramatic and its sunsets moving. Clifftoppers revel in theatrical effects.

in harmony with nature

Built to take advantage of the changing patterns of the water and the movements of the sun, moon and stars, this Australian house seems to float on the land.

THIS PAGE The lush vegetation around the house is a prominent feature of the property – large windows right up to the roof mean that the treetops are incorporated into the decor. The whole building is the result of a happy marriage between enterprising clients and a clever architect.

OPPOSITE The Reeveses like to eat outdoors whenever the weather is fine. They are both enthusiastic cooks and entertainers, so they decided to have a kitchen that led out onto an open-air area where they could cook and feed guests all summer.

I f we could produce a wish-list for the perfect waterside house, it would be somewhere we could live at ease surrounded by nature. It would be a house so flexible that we could enjoy it privately or with others in all of its moods: breakfast as the early sun rises over the water; lunch under the shade of trees with cool breezes moving the branches; and evening meals enjoyed with friends while watching the sun descend as the stars come out.

Fantasy? Maybe not, for – remarkably – this seems to be what the architects Peter Stutchbury and Sue Harper have achieved for their clients Robert Reeves and Gabby Hunt, as they then were. The house was built for them before they married – and their wedding was held there. 'We had the wedding two weeks after moving in,' says Gabby Reeves, 'and a party for sixty.'

Their house at Clareville on Pittwater, the most northerly peninsula around Sydney, seems to be part of the landscape, because that is what they asked for. 'The house is very open,' says Gabby, 'with the inside and outside all one space.' The kitchen – state of the art, because she owns a café and Robert is a food and menu consultant – juts out onto an open terrace, so they can cook out of doors in the summer. 'Robert cooks a lot and so do I. It's great for entertaining.'

Clareville may not have seemed so appealing at first. The architects describe the original site as cold, dark and wet. As a result, the living space had to be lifted up to get the best of the view and 'experience

the warmth and freedom of beach-house living'. The water around was landscaped to create a magnificent river, which rambles down the valley and back into Pittwater below. The view, however, was always superb since the site is on the north-eastern slope of the beach amphitheatre looking out to Pittwater itself.

Superb, too, were Stutchbury's clients, described by him as 'a magnificent couple, full of life, exuberance and generosity – welcoming, entertaining, vivacious, free, practical, open-minded, experimental, direct, no fuss'. Such paragons got the best that the architects could produce: a simple but ingenious building that is at once tranquil, transparent and stylish.

The house is arranged on several sloping levels, with the private part, designed for sleeping and seclusion, underneath. This area also adds the necessary height to the main floors and terraces where all the fun happens. The main area is designed to be completely adaptable, which means using the latest technology in a way that is both simple and complex. The lighting, for instance, is generally hidden – recessed into the tops of walls or inside cavities and under benches. This means that it is very adaptable. Heating is equally clever, with a solid-concrete floor and concrete walls that heat up during the day in winter and give out heat at night. In summer the floors and walls act as coolers, while the roof is inclined up to the north and down to the west to encourage sunlight to flood in during winter and stay out in summer. The steel-framed doors and windows are bolted in place, so they can be dismantled and put elsewhere.

There are many terraces around the house, making it seem part of the environment; meals can be taken where the view is best at any one time. And the landscaping, by Phoebe Pape, ensures that the trees and flora all around Clareville are part of the design. 'We have had kookaburras come into the house – in one door and out the next,' says Gaby. 'We've had them sitting on the backs of chairs, watching us and joining in by tucking into the oysters when we've had oysters and champagne at lunch. There are also lorikeets, galahs and cockatoos all around us.'

ABOVE AND RIGHT Even the bedrooms and bathrooms appear to be part of the natural slopes outside – and all the chairs and lounging areas are turned towards the stupendous views.

TOP LEFT AND TOP RIGHT Robert and Gabby spend a lot of time on the water or exploring nearby beaches in search of beautiful objects. Shells, water-eroded pebbles and shards of green glass, delicately etched by the salt water, adorn every room.

ABOVE LEFT An enormous conical vase draws attention to the view at the end of a white hallway.

The idea for the house came to them when they decided to have a family. 'We moved here because it would be right for children. We wanted to be near water, and there's a little beach – perfect for picnics.' Their first child, Ruby, was born in October 2000.

'It was a damp 1940s house before, and we spent a lot of time getting the feel for the place. It was in a gulley, but it's now all lifted up.' All around are native spotted gum trees and lemon-scented gums, some of which had to be cut down when the house was built. But the Reeveses planted 20 more of the fast-growing trees to surround them. 'They are growing really well. The light is now fantastic at any time of the day. The trees start as silhouettes, and at the end of the day we see the sunsets.'

The pair do a lot of kayaking, as well as wandering along the beaches collecting shells and paddling in the pools, when they aren't entertaining friends.

enhancing an exotic landscape

In a wild and sensuous setting overlooking the Pacific Ocean, one of Australia's most influential architects has created for himself a weekend home made of stone and timber, and carved on three levels into the side of a cliff.

Philip Cox is an important Australian architect who concentrates for the most part on mega-projects – which is sad for adventurous Australian home-owners because, as his own weekend home demonstrates, his domestic work is at once beautiful, clever, subtle and understated.

The house on Whale Beach amply demonstrates Philip Cox's attitude to domestic architecture: 'When designing houses for other people, which I don't do particularly often because I'm working on large-scale projects, I consider the landscape the most important feature, having regard to the client's brief. I believe in the philosophy of genius loci – if the architecture is correct, it's an enhancement of the landscape.'

In the case of Whale Beach, Cox was, of course, his own client – and he devised a brief for himself. His intention was to build a comfortable family weekend home where he could, if the desire took him, entertain up to a hundred people. The house was also required to double as a workplace and as a statement of his own design imperatives – in particular, his approach to the use of materials and what the Australian magazine

Vogue Living described in 1990 as 'his consummate ability to relate a building to its landscape in the most civilized and harmonious way'.

The landscape around Whale Beach is – at least to this non-Australian – exotic, wild and sensuous. The beach is the most northerly in the metropolitan area of Sydney, only 15 km from the city's central business district. Philip uses it as a retreat because he has a townhouse in the city: 'In Australian terms they're called crash pads – one- or two-bedroom apartments on Sydney Harbour.' This one is in part of a major development by the Cox Group on King Street Wharf.

Whale Beach could not be more different. 'It is called that because the headland resembles a whale,' explains Philip. 'Within the shore in front of the house we frequently have visits from whales, especially during September, when they're en route to their summer holiday in the Antarctic. A few years ago we were able to witness one of these beauties giving birth to a whale calf. They are also majestic and are growing in numbers again as a result of the whale-hunting moratorium.'

Philip's house is perched on cliffs high above the water. 'The house is in a bushland setting of banksia trees and eucalyptus, with panoramic views of the northern coastline and the Hawkesbury river. The view is dominated by a peninsula of sand, known as Barrenjoey, which has a lighthouse on its rocky outcrop. The house was designed in response to the site, the surrounding landscape, the water, the sun, all those things. Also the view – looking down at the rocks, looking up and down the coast, looking ahead. I wanted to make an interesting space here for an informal living experience.'

The house is designed on three levels: the upper one is a sun deck with entry hall and studio, where Philip works when he is not in Sydney. The middle level has all the main rooms – the living room and dining room, kitchen, library and main bedroom. 'The whole has an expansive feeling of space opening onto spacious verandas and decks. All the windows and doors are full-height glass, allowing the maximization of the view so, when you are in these spaces, the Pacific blue

horizon is always apparent.' The final, bottom level has extra bedrooms for guests, with their own sitting rooms. These, in turn, open onto their own verandas, and look out on the ocean through a screen of trees.

The house is constructed from timber and stone and, he says, 'has the appearance of floating lightly across the landscape'. *Vogue Living* agreed: 'The main part of the house is roofed with that characteristic Cox trademark, vaulted white corrugated steel which drifts from one height to another with graceful languor. The top deck is paved with ceramic tiles in the palest of greens (as in Cox's National Maritime Museum) and partly screened from the sun by the curved sweep of a lightweight tensioned fabric stretched over a white steel frame.'

Extraordinarily, this complex structure was built in no time. 'Twelve months from go to whoa,' says Philip Cox. It was added to an existing Bauhaus-type building, but that probably made the construction more time-consuming than building from scratch. 'I used the roof of it and added this and that,' he comments modestly. No house can be seen from the building, and – since it is surrounded by a nature reserve, and therefore carefully planned – it, in turn, can barely be seen from the beach below.

'There is no garden in the English tradition,' Philip explains. 'The garden is natural bushland of the most extraordinary textures of fallen leaves and branches with pale-pink trunked angophora lanceolate trees, which have the appearance of stark-naked bodies. Hairy candled banksias are the other dominant species, so the total picture is one of an untouched wilderness.' Banksias are named after Sir Joseph Banks, who sailed with Captain Cook in the *Endeavour* in 1768. He collected many specimens of Australian flora, and the pressed banksia flowers remain in the Natural History Museum's collection in London.

In this wilderness there are koala bears, possums, lizards and snakes. 'Snakes are particularly dangerous in Australia, but they usually get out of your way on approach. The problem is accidentally stepping on them. There is a haunting beauty in snakes, especially the redbelly black snake and the green-and-brown diamond python. However, we don't have kangaroos as we are too metropolitan.'

The house is, of course, a retreat, but that does not make it a place that encourages somnolence. Philip and his partner, the journalist Janet Hawley, come here to recharge their batteries and those of the five children they have between them – Janet's Sam,

Ben and Kim, and Philip's Charlotte and Sophie. This is where they sail, surf and go bushwalking – 'all the things typical Australians like doing', says Philip.

'The water is intense Pacific blue, and I can look from the veranda down onto the rock ledges below and the changing colours of the ocean with its reefs and sand beds. For most of the year, the Pacific rollers come crashing across the rocks below, so there is enormous dynamism and interest created at the very foot of the house.

'I entertain often here because the environment is very stimulating. The upper level of the house is partially enclosed by a translucent cover so that, throughout the year, we are able to enjoy the temperate climate and a two-way view either of the ocean or the bushland behind.

'Light is a most important part of the design. The roof has glazed strips with controllable louvre systems allowing the penetration of winter sun into the house while excluding summer sun. The result of this is the fascinating shadows and the drama of cloud changes within the house.

'Living in the Whale Beach house is romantic: being able to watch the moon rise over the vast Pacific Ocean, sending its silver reflections across the rippling waves. We watch the sun set over the hills of the nearby national park. The hills turn indigo and the sky a deep orange. The romance of the light is the most intriguing sensation.'

THIS PAGE The plain living room with its huge fireplace and prominent chimney is coloured all in neutrals, with picture windows looking out over the large veranda.

OPPOSITE A row of casual but comfortable director's chairs have been positioned around the veranda to allow observers to catch all the action that goes on – once a whale gave birth to a calf outside the windows.

Breton chic on a high point

This romantic creeper-clad house, bathed in the subtle, seductive light of France's north-west coast stands high on a rocky bluff softened by quantities of evergreen and deciduous native trees.

Coastal light always attracts artists. Schools of painters have established themselves at the Cornish seaside resorts of St Ives and Newlyn; painters, poets and musicians were drawn to Naples in the 18th century; in California, David Hockney has found the brilliant light to be an inspiration, as Gauguin did in the South Sea islands.

There are many places along the French coast that have contributed hugely to how we see things today. Matisse and Dufy couldn't get enough of the vibrant quality of the Mediterranean light on the Riviera, while late 19th-century artists, including the Impressionists, loved the charms of the north-west coast.

It is on that very coast, near St Malo, that Laurence Sabouret and her husband, Yves, spend their holidays and weekends – and it is the light there that inspires them, too. Laurence tells of Picasso's visits to the area and how she loves walking along the beaches where, a century ago, he walked and got ideas for his paintings.

The northern light is more subtle than the bright light of the Mediterranean. The sky is often overcast and cloudy, providing the shadowless effect that artists strive for in their north-facing studios. The colours are more subdued and the contrasts less violent, and the overall touch of mist and rain is evocative of days spent walking briskly along the sands, hearing the cries of the seabirds combating the gales, searching for objects washed up among the rollers.

Laurence and Yves, with their children Louis-Benoît, Paul and Victoire, come here from Paris, experiencing a complete change from sophistication to rurality that provides a welcome relief from the constant stress of the city. They way they do so is extremely French. Not for them the barbecues on the beach and the shorts and flip-flops that characterize Australian waterside living – nor do they follow British ideas of superior camping. While the Americans treat their holiday homes as ideal for outdoor entertaining, the French

ABOVE On a veranda high above the sea is a charming dining area, where a simple striped cloth covers a table laid with local food and wine. A tiny model of a yacht adds extra charm. Real yachts in the bay below are an integral part of the wonderful view.

OPPOSITE AND BELOW Its steeply sloping slate roof and characteristic 'gothick' silhouette place this house indisputably in France, and, although the climate can be as balmy as on the coast of the Mediterranean, the style is typical of the Atlantic coast of Brittany. The family do not devote a great deal of time to gardening – instead, they allow the native plants to cover the steep cliffs.

are not willing to give up formality, the *comme il faut* of daily life. If the holiday home is to be enjoyed, it must be done so with rules.

Built about 100 years ago, the Sabourets' house is typical of the *balnéaire* architecture found all along the coast – 'inherited from the Normandy example seen at Deauville but with a typically Breton twist', says Laurence. In the salon the walls are covered with oak *boiseries* [panelling] and there is a large fireplace, also in oak, carved with Breton motifs. The building's high and spiky roof is covered in steely slates, with large red chimneys poking up and through. The windows have charming louvred shutters which give protection against the hot sun in summer and the storm-force winds that howl around in winter.

The view from the terrace is stupendous: framed by the branches of pines and the rocky outcrops is the sea, dotted in summer with scores of yachts. During the day the scene is almost unreal in its beauty, while at night, one by one, the lights of the boats flicker on.

Laurence Sabouret has been very clever in bringing the scene below into the decor of the house above. She has not been tempted to paint over the heavy colour of the oak panelling, whose arched fields are repeated both in the large doors themselves and in the arches above the doors of the hall. It would have made the house lighter, even more fashionable, to have done so, but its character would have been lost.

Where Laurence has made changes, they all relate to the house's clifftop position. For example, the colours used throughout the house are virtually restricted to shades of cream and white with brilliant sea blues and turquoises. It could be the Caribbean, the Riviera or a sun-filled Greek island that is being conjured up by the evocative, ubiquitous sea blues. To emphasize this illusion, the railings of the terrace and its floor are all painted a sharp white, while the decor is nautical: a red-and-white striped tablecloth with a deep fringe is laid with blue glasses to match the sea, a bunch of

OPPOSITE Very few patterns are allowed to detract from the essential drama of the views from the windows – and the presence of the sea is constantly evoked with groupings of limpet, mussel, scallop and cockle shells, sea-washed pebbles, simple white decoy birds and collections of transparent blue-glass candlesticks, flower vases and lamps.

wild flowers found on the beach and a little model yacht. Behind is a lifebelt with the house's name painted on. For siesta time there are plenty of deck loungers made of teak, their comfortably raked backs and foot-rests cushioned with off-white cotton. An awning provides shade from the sun on hot days.

Indoors from the terrace is a main living area, where the colours are also brilliant blue and various shades of white. Sofas have soft white covers piped in blue and are set on a diaper-patterned rug in exactly the same colours. On the white covers are blue cushions and others in the sort of Indian fabric that, 300 years ago, arrived in Marseilles from the East and promptly became Provençal. To these elements add white-painted cabriole-legged French tables, covered with seawashed shells and a collection of cerulean-blue glass, models and paintings of yachts, and white Roman blinds – and you have a room that combines, in one go, sophistication, comfort and the seaside.

The same colours are repeated in the main bedroom – white curtains, a blue diaper wallpaper, blue-and-white bed linen and even a little blue-and-white fabric box, while elsewhere Provençal tablecloths and blue-and-white European and Chinese ceramics are teamed with navigational charts, more seagoing pictures and even blue-and-white carpet bowls.

The Sabourets' house is given over to holidays and entertaining, always within the rules. 'When the house is *complet*, there must always be half children and animals, half friends.'

The cooking for the guests is taken seriously. 'The chef – Yves – and I speak together from the morning to the evening, and after all the meals, to decide on the meal to come next. We analyse the one just finished, point by point: the cooking, the heat of the oven, duration, the aspect of the meat brought to table, its presentation, decoration – and how to do better. The *maîtresse de maison* is a Libra, so I always say, "half, half" – balance the diet, share in equal part

'All the decoration is devoted to the sea. Blue for the curtains, the same West Indies blue that you can see through the pine trees when the weather is beautiful. The sea can be like a blue lagoon.'

meat, fish, eggs, *entremets* (sugar or salted) on the week. I want the *feuilletés* of the tart to be as light as the sea air floating on the terrace; when weighed, it is just a feather. Red fruit or apricots are bought from Monsieur Collet, who gets fresh vegetables and fruits every day. We frequently have a *potage* for dinner. *Potage Breton aux légumes* is one of our favourites: salted butter in the casserole, vegetables cut into dice. Turn them about for ten minutes then cover them in water – of course, we use the natural mineral water, which comes from a place only 15 km away.'

From the moment when the Sabourets wake up in the morning, there is a timetable for the day, even at weekends. 'In the morning, from my bedroom window – we take our breakfast in bed – I chat with the breakfasters on the terrace. The terrace is our "living room" and the meeting point for everybody. The terrace is full south – it's so hot that we wear Breton hats with straw and a velvet ribbon. They read the newspapers that we get at seven-thirty.'

Next is the question of what everyone will eat – a major French preoccupation. 'I do the shopping list with Yves, the chef. I bend from the balcony like a diva in a theatre, with the terrace and the long sandy beach and the musical sound of the water on the rocks, and we argue about the menu.'

By 9.30 her daughter, Victoire, has to be at school. 'We say goodbye on the terrace, then she goes underneath it to take the path to the stairs to the beach. She opens the door to the stairs and my Jack Russell terrier, Big Ben, comes back from his one hour of jogging on the beach between eight and nine.

THIS PAGE AND OPPOSITE Since the Breton house has a strong character all its own, the owners have disciplined their input. The colours are confined to soft neutral shades enlivened with bright sea blues, navy and other primary colours. The living room has blue curtains, blue-piped sofas with creamy covers and cream Roman blinds. In good weather the French windows are kept open to allow in the salty sea air. Deck loungers are made with plain wood and cream fabrics, while the lifebuoys are a bit of fun rather than a reliable form of life-saving equipment.

My labrador, Dundee, is already lying on the terrace waiting for me and the eleven o'clock sea bathe.' Before that – by ten o'clock, says Laurence – if the weather is fine, the cushions on the wooden chairs, the beach towels and the parasol are ready for the morning's sunbathing. But there are still regulations to be enforced. 'I forbid sun oil outside the bathroom (unless they are hidden away in a *trousse*) and I forbid topless – there is the beach for that. I approve of a nice *tenue*.' Of course.

So, as the morning proceeds, Yves and Laurence, their children and guests arrive on the terrace, carefully dressed for a day by the seaside. Although topless is forbidden *chez Sabouret*, bathing outfits are allowed in the morning.

By lunch, guests and family must have changed again into something a bit less casual. 'At lunchtime, no more bathing suits on the terrace. There should be an adequate conversation – sports, weather, cooking.' A siesta is allowed in the shadows after lunch before *goûter* is made for the children at 4.30. This may consist of '*le célèbre gâteau Breton, les craquelins et les crêpes dentelles*'.

I rather approve of this structured approach to the day. How many times have stays with friends been ruined by meals running hours late and sometimes not even turning up at all? Nothing like that can happen at the Sabourets' house.

Following the siesta and *goûter*, there is a pause before guests assemble for yet another meal. Between 7.15 and 7.30 everyone is back on the terrace for cocktails and fruit juices. This will include those who have ignored the siesta in favour of golf, for there is an 18-hole golf course nearby. 'The 16th, 17th and 18th holes are links, made on the sand, and we play along the beach.'

But by 7.30 it is time to admire the view and the position. 'The light at seven-thirty is wonderful, pure, gentle for the eyes. The rocks are burning in red and rose, and the air is suspended. The terrace is a boat, diving in the sea, it is the *vigie* which announces the weather. The French flag streams in the wind.'

It could, indeed, come straight from one of those 19th-century paintings – a Renoir, perhaps, or a charming corner of an exterior by Vuillard.

THIS PAGE AND OPPOSITE The ground floor of the house is designed and decorated very much in the bourgeois French manner, with heavy panelling and ornate arched doors in the hallway. The panelling in the dining room is even grander. The Sabourets updated the decor by introducing smart ships' portraits, maritime maps and models of boats. The family use the house for entertaining – making good use of their blue-and-white Breton pottery and napkins in the same shades, while even the knives and forks have blue handles.

a lighthouse keeper's cottage

A keeper's cottage beside the lighthouse that inspired the artist Edward Hopper to paint one of his most distinctive views has been transformed into a family home without damage to its iconic significance.

ABOVE A distinctive group of buildings on the rugged coast of Maine, centred on a lighthouse and the keeper's home, became very well known when Edward Hopper painted it in the 20th century. The still-working lighthouse is visible between the main house and a folly. There are about 4,800 km (3,000 miles) between this lonely light and the next landfall to the east.

LEFT At the centre of the keeper's cottage is a stairwell that is lit from above to give illumination and airiness throughout the building.

Since Pliny the Elder wrote on the subject in the first century AD, living by water for the fun of it has been regarded as the preserve of the rich. Yet poor people live by water, too. Their role has been to harvest the seas or to maintain the fishponds, to use waterpower for milling and weaving, to live beside fertile coasts when the earth inland is a desert, to look after sea defences and dams – and to guard and protect all those who, from prehistory, have travelled by water and sea. Ferrymen,

coastguards, lifeboats and lighthouses are not new. Around 280 BC there was a lighthouse on the island of Pharos, off Alexandria in Egypt – one of the seven wonders of the ancient world. Lighthouses are always dramatic. They are located on headlands and either side of harbour mouths, on dangerous rocks in dangerous seas, and on islands where the tides swirl sandbanks in different directions twice a day. They also represent landfall, a beacon of light in an uncertain world; they offer the hope of safety.

Cape Elizabeth Light is a famous lighthouse – not because it was built by the Lighthouse Stevensons, known for their unwreckable towers and for spawning the writer Robert Louis Stevenson; nor was it like the Longstone lighthouse, where, in 1838, the young Englishwoman Grace Darling helped her father rescue shipwrecked sailors from the steamship *Forfarshire*. This lighthouse and the keeper's house at its base were immortalized by the American artist Edward Hopper (1882-1967), who won lasting renown for, in particular, his scenes of lonely town life.

Cape Elizabeth Light does not represent town life, but it is certainly an example of the loneliness that can be found on any American coast or, indeed, on any coast around the world. The remote spots chosen for lighthouses may mean safety for sailors in foundering vessels, but for the lighthouse keeper and his family they represent duty above company, service before society, isolation for an income.

This particular lighthouse stands at the opening of Casco Bay, which lies at the head of Portland Harbour in Maine. It is located in an area of Cape Elizabeth known as 'Two Lights' because in 1874 two lighthouse towers were built about 300 metres apart to help sailors to distinguish these lights from those of nearby lighthouses.

THIS PAGE AND OPPOSITE Waterside dwellers often have a pair of binoculars or a telescope trained towards the view. This clifftop house overlooks busy shipping lanes and migratory routes for sea birds. The silhouette of the lighthouse can be seen from many rooms in the house, but, because of its height, the circling beam passes above the roof – so it doesn't keep anyone awake at night. To enhance the character of their home, the owners have introduced compasses, chronometers and seafarers' instruments.

Only one lighthouse remains active, though the other still stands. They are sited to be visible by all shipping in the area, but, unlike those in the Mediterranean, about 4,800 km (3,000 miles) from the nearest landfall – across the Atlantic. When the working lighthouse was automated, the small, century-old keeper's cottage that shelters below it against the winds became redundant.

The present owner of the keeper's cottage (but not of the lighthouse itself) came upon it by accident. Or that's how it seemed. 'I grew up in the nearby town,' he says. 'My family lived there for two generations. I was visiting my parents several years ago and decided to go to the ocean to look at the waves – there had been a huge storm. When I drove by the house, which I'd known all my life, I saw a "For Sale" sign. I was just amazed. So I immediately called the broker – and I was lucky enough to purchase the house. It wasn't anything I'd been planning. It wasn't even a decision. I just knew, instinctively, that it was what I wanted.'

THIS PAGE AND OPPOSITE A landing leads from the stairwell into the bedroom of one of the owner's daughters. The girl's little rag doll has been tucked up under the coverlet, which has quilted circles reminiscent of sea urchins and shells. Table lamps have been adapted from old sea lanterns or hurricane lamps.

Apart from his three young daughters, the owner has many relatives in the area, and he wanted to enlarge the house so it was possible to fit them all in. But this famous national symbol also had to continue looking as it did in Hopper's painting. So he hired the architectural firm of Stephen Blatt to make the changes.

'Cape Elizabeth Light is one of the most recognizable symbols of Maine's maritime history,' says Blatt. 'Our challenge was to nearly double its size in order to meet his family's needs, take better advantage of the spectacular ocean views and, at the same time, remain sensitive to the historical character of the building. In the interior, we were asked to make the humble lightkeeper's house, which had been insensitively renovated over the years, into one befitting a whaling captain.

'Our solution left the two most public views of the building largely intact. Much of the expansion – including a two-car garage with exercise room above, connecting hall and deck, and screened porch – was placed on the least publicly visible portion of the site. The existing utilitarian basement was also expanded downward and outward to create extra living space on this tight site. The main floor features a dramatic, open-plan two-storey oval rotunda capped by a triangular skylight. The second floor has three children's bedrooms and a master bedroom, all of which open onto the skylit rotunda.

'Interior finishes include antique heart-pine flooring, Douglas fir ceilings and extensive painted woodwork. Careful attention was paid to exterior historical detail – all the trims, including decorative rake-boards, were milled to match the existing profiles.'

Blatt took great care to match new stone with the weathered older walls, and the whole was landscaped so that it sat comfortably on its site.

It has been a terrific success for the owner. 'It is very much in keeping with the style and tradition of the old building,' he says. 'It's a truly amazing spot, high up on a hill. The view is as much about the sky, which is incredible, as it is about the ocean. We have a 360-degree view from the high point of the area, a place which just happens to be on the migratory route for birds. We get ducks, geese and wildfowl flying over – any bird that migrates.'

The lighthouse itself is, of course, part of this view. 'It's amazingly romantic and charming. In summer, on a clear night, you can sit and watch the light turning silently and serenely – and, at other times, see it in a

raging storm. The light is high enough to shine over the top of the house so the beam doesn't bother us. Then, from that point, you can see three other lights along the coast. Ships are passing all the time, fishing boats, pleasure boats, cruise ships. We're in a position to see the weather systems coming in over the ocean – a low front appears long before it reaches us and you can see thunderheads arriving, too.'

The family appreciates the history of their house: 'There have been only five keepers and their families living here in the hundred years since the house and light were built. We have discovered their old tools and logbooks. We still have grandchildren of the keepers come to the door and tell us about growing up in the house. This whole area of Maine is rich in maritime history – during the Civil War, 60 per cent of the shipping tonnage was owned by Maine shipowners, and the whole area was a very important trading post.'

Now the house is a second home – but one greatly loved and much used. 'My sister and parents, aunts and uncles all live nearby. We're up here all the time with our children. At Thanksgiving, for example, we had a dinner party for twenty-five. We do any kind of activity you can think of – cross-country and downhill skiing, boating, hiking and camping.'

'It's amazingly romantic and charming. In summer, on a clear night, you can watch the light turning silently and serenely – and, at other times, see it in a raging storm.'

Originally, Stephen Blatt explains, the whole idea of extending and changing this famous house caused a great deal of controversy among architectural preservationists. 'The end product is a testament to the notion that historic buildings can successfully evolve with changing times and lifestyles.' If they don't, I would add, there's no hope for them but an existence as a sterile museum. But, in this instance, the combination of architect and owner has created a living family home which not only gives pleasure to the present generation but also secures a viable future for Cape Elizabeth Light and the keeper's cottage for their second century.

THIS PAGE AND OPPOSITE The main bedroom has panoramic views over the clifftops to the busy sea lanes below. Everything – walls, woodwork and beamed ceilings – is painted white to enhance the effect of the waves and ripples of water below. Here, as elsewhere, the colours are kept to a single strong blue, with the only pattern being a bedcover of mixed shells. Given the strong character of the exterior, the owners have collected little lighthouses and Hopper artefacts such as books and stamps. as well as green glass objects to recall seawashed bottles.

beachside living

Living by a beach is like being on holiday all year round. You can get up at dawn and walk along sands wet with the tide and busy with wading birds; at noon you can watch the world go by from the vantage of your own veranda; at night you can watch the sun go down and the moon glinting on the waves.

life's a Long Island beach

For busy, harassed city-dwellers, nothing could be more therapeutic than to escape to this secluded corner of New England, where the beach remains the focal point of community life throughout the long days of summer.

THIS PAGE AND OPPOSITE Her father calls Elena Colombo's house, part of a Long Island community, 'that shack'. Well, it is a shack – but in the nicest possible way. It has survived the seas for more than a century and suits the locals' friendly lifestyle. The houses here were built as homes for workers at a nearby brick factory, and the new owners work hard to keep them simple. Being part of a fixed group of friends, however, means there is lots of easy entertaining too.

There is something about living beside water that attracts opposite extremes. At one end of the spectrum is the person who loves solitude and contemplation and is inclined to a certain reclusiveness – why go anywhere else if you have tranquillity and beauty all around? At the other end are those who desire to share their luck with family and friends. To some extent, the attitude varies according to the kind of waterside place that's chosen. It's easier to be alone on a clifftop or beside a still lake than it is to be alone by a beach. Ever since the Victorians took the plunge in their bathing machines, beaches have been about holidays, fun, children, expeditions and parties.

There could not be a better example of the beach as the focal point in the life of a community than Elena Colombo's chosen place on the shores of eastern Long Island, only two hours' drive from the centre of New York City. It is one of 31 old cottages that make up an entire community. This is not a community that consists simply of an informal group of people and houses like, say, a village or a block of flats; this is a legally grouped commune that owns common land and has a ruling board voted in to make decisions. The cottages were built about a century ago to house workers in a brick factory. By all accounts the workers didn't stay very long – perhaps because, in winter, this can be a fierce place where neither warmth nor running water can survive the frozen pipes.

When the family that ran the brick business realized that it could not keep workers in its tied cottages, it began to find holiday tenants, drawn to the area by the proximity of the burgeoning city of New York. 'It became a recreational summer home very soon after it was built,' says Elena. 'The brickworks has gone – it's now a marina – but bricks are still washed up all over the beaches and the shore. We gather them to make

> 'I can hardly start to expound on the positives of living by the water. The smell, the colours, the opportunity to sit and watch the birds, the sailboats, the fresh fish, the sun, the breeze.'

patios and walkways – so, in theory, the brickworks are still with us.' The cluster of cottages continued to be owned by the original family until a few years ago.

'Two New York developers came and spoke to the owners and made them a bid. When they told me and the other tenants that they were thinking of selling, we panicked. We organized ourselves into a motley crew and found a way of making a down payment and buying the property. The owners kept five of the cottages. Some tenants had to leave, but most of us managed to buy our homes. It was a very disruptive period for all of us.'

The present situation is that most people who live here own their houses – some of which are rented out to holidaymakers – but 36 hectares of land around the houses are communally owned, each owner having the equivalent of a shareholding in the total. All the community members are therefore allowed to walk wherever they please, other than in the small garden plots alongside the houses.

'I am currently on the board – in charge of road maintenance,' says Elena, a sculptor, with an amazed chuckle. The board is responsible for keeping up the infrastructure, such as roads and walkways, and for deciding who will buy cottages as they come up for sale. 'We have a list of people who want to buy houses. People who buy have to be approved, voted in by all of the rest of us.'

This is less alarming than it might seem for, says Elena, the community is 'very, very casual – run like a cooperative. We all meet each other, have no restrictions, and people understand that. That's why we're such a diverse group.' The character of the community – verging on a hippy commune, she adds – is so definite that 'people either get it or they don't'.

OPPOSITE, ABOVE
Elena Columbo prides herself on using found objects to decorate the house. Some are picked up on the beach, others come from local thrift stores. In the front porch a wire salad shaker doubles as a wall sculpture and an oil lamp stands on a white table; flowery cushions are piled on a cheerful striped blanket.

OPPOSITE, BELOW The back porch demonstrates the powerful decorative effect that can be achieved by the artful arrangement of simple objects such as old candlesticks and tools.

Those who don't 'get it' probably don't want to join in anyway. Elena comments that her father is one of the latter, calling her beloved cottage 'that shack'.

This is purely a summer community, for the cottages are not 'winterized': there is insufficient insulation to keep rooms warm in winter, and the plastic water pipes are still inclined to freeze, which means no running water. People do venture out in the cold, but usually to rough it for a hot picnic in front of a warm fire or for a single night snuggled in goosedown.

So only in summer does the place come fully alive, which is why it has such a carefree holiday ambience. The cottages are of various sizes. Three of them are very large, each with a floor area of about 110 square metres, while the rest have only one or two rooms and total floor areas of about 28 square metres. Most are decorated, just like Elena Colombo's, with casual finds from the beach and the water, and from the small local stores. I get the impression that, rather than trying to outdo each other in acquiring special objects, members of this community compete to find the least expensive decor. 'My place isn't at all fancy. The decorations come from the thrift stores that benefit local charities such as the animal shelter. I am a sculptor, and I'm starting to dot my property with pieces inspired by the wind and water. I use metal, stone, wood and bone found on or near the property.

'Everybody does the same because a single shell on a shelf looks beautiful here. The houses are so simple, so old, with 12-pane windows and wainscoting put in at the turn of the century, that simple decoration suits them. People here regularly go to the dump [formally known as the town recycling centre] and the local antique shop for finds – and there's The Barn, where people take things they no longer want. Others will

go there to pick things up, so everything circulates. We're into the whole recycling vibe. There are yard sales, too, where everything is real cheap – five cents – and bartering is big. It's very catch-as-catch-can, and nobody wants to be elegant.'

Even Elena's dog was discovered on the shore. 'My old dog Lucky, who died here this summer, I adopted seven years ago (he was already living on the shore here) and he was loved by all. I sprinkled his ashes over the property so he will be there for ever. Everyone in the community came and paid their respects to him with pats, bones, bacon and love.

'What makes living by the water particularly special for me is the people I live next to and the reverence we have for our slice of paradise – not to mention the fact that when I open my eyes in the morning all I see is an uninterrupted view of the water.'

The owners are a diverse bunch. 'There are painters, photographers, people in the film industry, a woman who is on to her second screenplay, and a writer of children's books. There are decorators and designers, a psychiatrist and an acupuncturist, a massage therapist and antique dealers.' Elena thinks that if all the owners put out signs advertising what they could do, they would have access to every skill they might ever need.

'Many of us are friends from Manhattan, and we have gotten to know everyone and learned to live side by side. We have beautiful sparkly dinners out on the lawns, when we all bring something to eat and set up long tables. There are children and old people, gays and straights, blacks and whites – and everything in between. The oldest person is 85, and often the youngest has just been born. It is a true commune.

'There are spontaneous parties here all the time, when everybody goes to everybody else's place. One friend always brings fireworks, and another has an enormous grill – so we go to the local fish store and just throw the fish on the grill. It's possible to fish in our inlet. At five-thirty in the morning you'll see the boats chugging in the water out front. There's flounder and bluefish to be had and, in the bay, bass and blowfish – what we call chicken of the sea. There are mussels and clams and lobster out near the sound.'

Also not far from the shore you can find porgies, red snapper, swordfish, tuna and the tantalizingly named weakfish. Diamond-back sea turtles can be spotted in the water here, too.

Much of the land in the area is still farmed, and there are vineyards everywhere. 'There are miles and miles of grapes, and the vegetables grown around here probably supply the whole of the rest of Long Island.'

Elena Colombo has her own small garden, where she grows tomatoes, peppers, peas and beans with squashes in autumn. 'Everyone has a herb bed – the

ABOVE The main kitchen space doubles as a dining room with plain wooden table and chairs and, in one corner, an old round mirror above a high stool.

OPPOSITE The area around the original kitchen sink has been enlivened with daffodil-yellow walls and decorated with propped pictures and other items found at nearby thrift stores.

ABOVE Like an enormous galvanized bucket, the bath fits neatly into the minuscule bathroom, which is festooned with bright beach towels and primitive pictures.

LEFT When the weather is good, Elena prefers to take a shower outside.

BELOW Many of the rooms in the house retain their original features, such as wooden planks and built-in cupboards. The charm comes from Elena's clever use of painted walls and furniture.

plants seem to love it out here, perhaps it's the salty air.' And herbs are swapped among members of the community, too. 'I grew ten tomatoes this year – not a lot – but it was terrific to walk out and pluck one to make a salad and eat it on my own kitchen table.'

Messing about in boats is an integral part of life. 'There are a couple of boats owned by friends that we can all pile into and zip to another spot across the water to swim or picnic. Two are restored mahogany runabouts that match the property out here.'

Indeed, the whole community could not be less like the frenetic and famous Hamptons, which are close in distance but light years away in terms of atmosphere. 'New York has been obsessed with the Hamptons' glitz and glamour for so many years that no one paid any attention to the rest of the area. It just plodded on alone – even though it's warmer and sunnier here, no one can figure out why.' The Hamptons are now expensive, smart and overdeveloped; their loss has been this small community's gain. Elena is lyrical about it all. 'The light out here takes my breath away. The weather can change in an instant. We have everything from still, hot, humid days to driving hail and hurricanes. The cottages have weathered many storms, and sometimes it feels as if they are protected by a higher power, or maybe they were just built right.'

What is so special here is the feeling of shared responsibility and the pleasure that comes from being part of a close-knit group. It is like a family, but one whose members are chosen for their likemindedness. While they love the joint meals around the shore and the joys of meeting friends on holiday, they are also eager to take care of the environment. Hence everyone swaps household furniture and necessities, trawls the seashore for found objects, shells, driftwood and old fishing gear, and patronizes the charities' thrift stores.

Elena was concerned to ensure that I didn't reveal the exact location of this slice of paradise – everyone's privacy must be preserved, she said. I reckon that, if the owners of those 31 cottages have been clever enough to find a sanctuary where the pressures are minimal and the pleasures great, there is no good reason why I should disturb that. 'Whenever I come here, I just don't want to leave. I feel so lucky,' Elena says. Lucky, certainly – but luck has to be looked for.

ABOVE Original tongue-and-groove walls have been painted a soft white, as has the plain iron bedstead in Elena's bedroom. Elena has used her clever eye to add a simple table with an old-fashioned lamp to a single picture, an impressive straw hat and a wicker chair.

LEFT A guest bedroom has been decorated with sea-green beaded walls, and an old mirror has been propped between the beds. Although many articles have been retrieved from skips, the fan quilt was an exceptional buy.

LEFT From the sheltered area beside the pool a path leads directly to the beach. Heavy-leafed banana trees provide a shady respite from the relentless Caribbean sun.

RIGHT French windows allow the trade winds to flow through the main living area with its shell-upholstered chairs and stools. All the walls and floors are in the local cream coral stone and the furniture is chosen to mingle with its colours – and for its coolness.

elegance in the colonial style

The inspiration is the traditional vernacular style of the Caribbean island – that is, buildings built by local people, often without the involvement of an architect.

Colonial architecture evolved in Barbados and elsewhere in the West Indies when the English first arrived in the 17th century, originally as pioneers but with well-established views about the way houses should be built. As time went on, Barbados became settled by increasingly rich sugar planters, and with prosperity came the desire to import the elegant fashions sweeping Britain: the Italianate Palladian architecture with its strict rules of proportion, the latest invention of sash windows with good-sized panes of glass, and the furniture inspired by classical Greece and Rome. Heavily shaded verandas derived from another British colony, India. The settlers also borrowed from the Mediterranean notions of the

French who, along with the Spanish and Portuguese, had colonized other Caribbean islands. From the Mediterranean came jalousies – louvred shutters that kept out the glare of the sun while letting any breeze filter indoors – along with cold stone floors, corridors open from front to back to catch the winds, and a preponderance of white on walls, floors and ceilings.

It is this mixture of styles, which became typical of the Caribbean as a whole, that architect Larry Warren has captured so well in his houses in Barbados. He uses it both when restoring old buildings and when creating new houses for the fortunate people who can afford holiday homes on the island. Warren generally searches out those old houses that need his touch –

LEFT The guest bedroom, like many in these parts, has been designed to have its own balcony overlooking the sea. White louvred blinds and a latticed bedhead are combined with stark white walls to give a deliciously cool impression.

RIGHT The guest balcony follows through on the white theme, with white trellis arching over the veranda, white rush chairs arranged around a simple wooden table, and slanting louvres to take advantage of the trade winds. Beyond is a lush tropical garden.

he is determined to save what he can of the historic architecture – and, as a result, owns a couple himself. One of these properties, known as Waverley, has become a holiday home for visitors to Barbados. 'It consists of three town houses in the centre of Gibbs Bay, maybe the most desirable after the famous Sandy Lane,' he says. 'The town houses take their name from the original seaside residence that occupied the site.

'The architecture is a blend of the modern and the traditional stone architecture of the Barbadian homes of the Victorian era, which evolved from the wooden chattel house. Regrettably, these architectural gems are disappearing from Barbados's roadside scene.'

Waverley, as recreated by Warren, is a series of cool white rooms, some indoors, some on shaded verandas, some outside, where leafy palms and banana trees provide both shadow and splashes of emerald green against the neutrals of faded wood and coral stone. Even though space was tight, Warren was determined to give the houses vibrant tropical gardens. 'I put great emphasis on creating a private garden between the residence and the beach, with dense planting dividing the spaces. This has given a pleasant shaded outdoor space for residents and their children, who can safely play in the garden area.' From the main living space, which includes both dining and sitting rooms, there is a cool covered and paved area which gives directly onto the blue waters of the pool with its bar and barbecue.

From this water it is only a short walk along a path to the beach itself which, like many on Barbados, is a vision of white sand, soothing palm trees and clear deep-blue water. 'As with most upmarket property along the west coast of the island, frontage is limited, so it was quite an exercise to provide three bedrooms and two bathrooms along with a small plunge pool and spacious living areas – all within a 22-foot frontage. The interior is a blend of coral stone walls, plaster floors and bleached pine and local carved stone, with a collection of paintings by local artists.'

Larry Warren's wife, Anna, designed the inside of Waverley. 'The interiors reflect a collection of my wife's taste and our lifestyle. For example, the formal dining room is for special occasions, but it also serves as a place where Anna can display some of her collections of furniture and accessories. Anna has very good taste

'The residence is not pretentious but simple and to the point. The main living area is a large veranda surrounding an outdoor coral stone room facing west to the sea.'

THIS PAGE AND OPPOSITE Larry Warren's designs contrive to develop the Barbadian vernacular style, which was inspired by Georgian Britain, ante-bellum America, colonial India and Spain. Jalousies, cool cut stonework, deep verandas and generous windows introduce tropical touches to a classical foundation.

– at least, I think so.' That is evident from her calm interiors at Waverley. Virtually everything is white, but a clever and sophisticated series of different shades of white. Exterior doors and shutters look antique and distressed, their old white paint just slightly lighter than the beautiful soft creams of the coral stone. Woodwork, such as the lattice work around the plain

stone veranda pillars and the louvred jalousies that keep the sun from the outdoor rooms, is softly grey. Mirror frames are brushed with white, and white tiles line the white bath, with white fluffy towels slung over a white bathrail.

Occasionally white gives way to a cool blue, as in the main living room, where the comfortable wicker chairs have cushions upholstered in a fabric scattered with blue tropical shells, and the cushions on the dining chairs mirror the blue Bristol glass on the table and the striped rugs on the floor. Shells and fish are a recurrent theme.

It is important when decorating a house for holiday visitors that the local style is used throughout. If you are visiting Barbados, you don't want to feel that the rooms are standardized hotel decor. Waverley certainly avoids the mundane in favour of the old colonial traditions which make so much sense on a tropical island with its drenching storms and debilitating heat.

an English rural idyll

Panoramic views of sea and sky combine with the rolling landscapes of the Weald and the South Downs and the intriguing wetlands of Romney Marsh to create a stunning location for this 1950s house.

Philip Hooper is a man who, I would guess, does not wax lyrical all that easily. But here he is talking about Beach House, perched above a shingle beach outside Hastings, on the south coast of England: the place where William the Conqueror landed in 1066, and near where the last English king, Harold, lost his final battle and his life – a place resonant with history.

'It's a constantly changing panorama. The sea is always different. Just now it's a milky turquoise, and the sky is just turning pink with dusk. There are clouds on the horizon, but above us the sky is still pale blue. Boats are constantly moving up and down because this coast is a major shipping route. We get container vessels and liners sailing past on the horizon. Lots of activity. This is also a light-aircraft route, so we have planes flying above us. The beach has lots of activity too: people going

THIS PAGE Beach House is a modern house in a historic setting, close to the site of the Battle of Hastings. The house exploits its dramatic position, with full-frontal views from every storey.

RIGHT An old car port has been converted into a cobbled outdoor dining area; the exotic and abundant garden diverts prying eyes.

THIS PAGE AND OPPOSITE Since film-maker Derek Jarman created his shingle garden overlooking a nearby shore in the 1980s, beachside gardening has undergone a revolution. This garden incorporates many of Jarman's motifs, including sea-washed pebbles, cork floats, flotsam and jetsam, but Philip Hooper has unified it by using a background colour of pale turquoise with added dashes of brilliant cobalt as in his Moroccan bowls. The greyer shade of blue in the spiky agave plant, and the lilac-tinged scallop shells, complement the colours of the seashore.

along by the sea wall, windsurfing, kites, people walking their dogs. We can sit back and watch it all.' Philip and his partner, Alan Fergusson, have made their house into a comfortable observatory the better to see all this activity. Its main living room, which takes up the entire third floor, has glass windows all around, and an open balcony beyond. A black solid-fuel iron stove is in the perfect position for people to sit beside while beach-watching in winter and during the violent storms that occasionally lash this coast.

The house itself is almost certainly unique. It was designed in 1958 by Michael Patrick, an architect who was more a theoretician and teacher than a hands-on designer. The family who commissioned him to create this house (and who sold it to Philip Hooper a decade ago) believe that Patrick never built another house.

It is also curious in the context of the time when it was built. In 1958 Britain was still recovering from the Second World War and the austerity programmes that followed it. Most homes built during that period were strictly practical – which this house is not. 'It is more reminiscent of American houses than British ones,' says Philip, an interior designer.

Unconventionally, the living room is at the top of the house because this is where the best views are. Each wall is made of glass, although only in the sea-facing wall does the glass reach from floor to ceiling. The other three walls have chest-high tongue-and-groove wooden dados with windows above. In 1950s style, the windows are shallow and wide. Philip fitted all of them with dark-pink Venetian blinds, also very 1950s, and painted the window frames a sea blue.

He also moved the main kitchen down to the ground floor, leaving only a serving kitchen – with fridge, hotplate, sink – in the room alongside the dining area. He has, however, kept all the 1950s room dividers, often with cupboards and sliding doors, and the unmistakable period character has been enhanced by the period furniture and decorations.

'I had two houses before, one in London and the other in Devon, which were Arts and Crafts in period, late Victorian. When I discovered this house I sold everything I had collected of that period at auction

and started again. The house is so strong that it needed strong things in it.' The furniture in the living room includes two Robin Day chairs, once upholstered in orange but now a soft donkey brown, and a daybed by Capellini. Everywhere there are pieces of 1950s pottery and brilliantly coloured Venetian glass. Many of the vases, bowls and lights are also by Italian and French designers. 'When I started collecting the 1950s, I thought English pieces were a bit bleak, so I went for French and Italian, which are more sexy.'

All the bedrooms and bathrooms are on the first floor. Originally there were four bedrooms, but one has become a dressing room. The bedrooms, all small, have been left as they were designed by Michael Patrick, who was clearly inspired by the interiors of ships and smaller yachts. The bedrooms have built-in bunks raised high above useful storage areas, and once again the windows provide splendid views.

Philip Hooper's house has far more than sea views. 'The back of the house faces onto the South Downs and their grazing sheep. It's very bucolic. I wanted it

for its 360-degree views as well as its proximity to the sea. We have the landscape of the Downs and the Weald, along with marshes, all in a small area. There are freshwater pools on Romney Marsh that are stopovers for migrating birds. On the beach there are oystercatchers, dunlins and wading birds.'

The ground floor is the least exciting part of the house, but an old car port has been turned into an outside dining area complete with nautical allusions, and the original cobbled floor remains below the table. Beyond it stretches an extraordinarily exotic garden – more Havana than Hastings – which, says Alan Fergusson, was designed partly to distract passers-by from peering into the 'goldfish bowl' of the house. Though it seems larger, it is only 20 metres long and 17 metres wide, but Philip's design both blocks the view and leads the eye onwards to the beach.

Running beside the outside dining area is a straight canal filled with colourful Koi carp. The sweeps of shingle beyond it are planted with the sort of spiky-leaved plants that can cope with such sharp drainage.

THIS PAGE AND OPPOSITE In keeping with the style of the 1950s – when this beachside house was built – virtually every wall has its wide, shallow windows. These vary from full-length ones, which give expansive views of England's south coast, to chest-high ones that look away from the sea, focusing attention inland, on the fields and hills beyond the garden. Philip is an avid collector of 1950s pottery, including works from Poole and Rye potteries, along with Venetian glass and period furniture.

THIS PAGE AND OPPOSITE Philip Hooper's house is a virtuoso display by an architect who appears never to have designed another domestic building. Since it was commissioned by the previous owners, virtually nothing has been changed. Philip has been astute enough to refer back to the 1950s with his spiky cactuses and windows shaded by Venetian blinds. Most of the fittings are original, and their character is emphasized by the displays of quirky art pottery of the period.

131

The bedrooms have been left as they were designed by Michael Patrick, who was clearly inspired by the interiors of ships and smaller yachts.

RIGHT The four bedrooms of the original house have been reduced to three. Each room is walled with tongue-and-groove wooden planks, and the beds are built in above storage areas so they are quite high off the ground and resemble ships' bunks.

ABOVE, BELOW AND FAR RIGHT Philip journeys all over the world and is quite unable to resist the shells and driftwood he finds on his travels. These are used to create the seaside garden, which is planted with spiky Mediterranean plants.

In the garden, yuccas and cordylines are underplanted with grey santolina and eschscholzia. Everywhere driftwood, standing upright, leads the eye towards the beach. These pieces have been dragged from the shingle beyond and decorated with shells and stones, which Philip brought back from travels all over the world. He also collects stones with holes running through them – fairy stones that are believed to bring luck. These are threaded onto clipped hawthorn bushes and appear only when the leaves are shed in autumn.

Many other plants are evergreen, with strongly shaped leaves and strong growth patterns, while other grey Mediterranean groupings are kept from flowering by clipping. The whole is sheltered by evergreen holm oaks and Scots pines along with tamarisk and *Euonymus japonicus*, which can survive sea winds.

In true beach mode, walls and furniture (some designed by Philip) are painted in bright blues and yellows. The garden designer John Brookes praises the garden for its 'essence of place'. It 'encompasses not only what will grow best in a given place without improvement but what, in terms of hard as well as soft materials, looks right there too. So, from the juxtaposition of its plants, overlaying a strong and simple design in a complex location, the owners have created something of real and lasting charm.'

huge skies and a world of white

Whiteness, brightness and simplicity are the main features of this 1920s house in the south of England, whose decor is inspired by the light, the sea and the shingle beach.

David Davies's weekend retreat is a splendid post-Lutyens building of bay windows, dormers and high chimneys dating from the 1920s. It sits, with tremendous presence, just behind the sea wall near Bexhill in Sussex. Between it and the pebbled beach is a formal garden of the Gertrude Jekyll type, which has been recreated by an influential English garden designer, Stephen Woodhams. The house has been updated by David himself, a well-known designer of shops and hotels but never – he laughs – houses. He wants to keep it that way because the house is a retreat from work. 'It's like The Priory to me, a detox centre from work. My friends all come here to detox from

ABOVE AND OPPOSITE, FAR LEFT The frames of the Edwardian mullioned windows have been painted matt white. Beside them are white upholstered day beds, white decoy birds and, on the mantelpiece, groups of exotic patterned shells from all over the world.

ABOVE RIGHT David often takes his holidays on the island of Sardinia, and it was there that he found the extraordinary dried twigs that sit in a shell-hung vase.

OPPOSITE, ABOVE Other drought-loving plants such as spiky aloes are put in white pots in front of the living-room fireplace to combine with furniture all covered in white and with dark wooden ceiling beams and floors.

work too because it's so relaxing. In London, where I live during the week, I can feel exhausted but not here – perhaps because there's nowhere to go.'

One thing that prompted David to buy was that he wanted to be near his parents. 'I had known the house for years, then my sister told me it was for sale. It was a wreck at the time. Although I'm originally from west London, my parents retired to Sussex, and I used to drive past this house on my way to see them – and dream about living in it. I couldn't believe it when it came on the market. I bought it straight away, but some people thought I was mad.

'The previous occupants had confused the interior by mixing busy wallpaper with deep-pile carpet. It was revolting – the whole place was like a 1950s box from hell. But I could see through that. It is a beautiful house really, and well planned. The true fabric of the building was pretty much untouched. I just had to take it back to its bare bones and start again.'

When he took up the carpets he found the original high-quality wooden floorboards that were a feature of the period. Then he painted everything else white – apart from the original panelling and beams in the

hall, living room and dining room. Not only the walls but also the window frames, ceilings, doors, shelves, furniture and light fittings are painted white. 'My house in London is all white too. I would love to have the gall to paint all the beams white, but I haven't yet. I used lots of different whites – Papers and Paints in London is particularly good on them.'

Where Bexhill has the advantage over London is with the wonderful light that comes from the huge skies and the sea below. Anyone who lives with water knows that each enhances the other: the sky brightens the sea, and the sea reflects more light back to the sky. 'I love the light and the patterns light casts,' says David. 'It's ironic that I use colour all the time in my job but can't cope with it away from work. I love the purity of white and, because of the Arts and Crafts influence, and being by the beach, I've used that along with woody textures and tones.'

One of the first things he did was to install double-glazing. The original 1920s windows were rotten and had to be replaced with new ones made to withstand the gale-force winds that are common by the sea. I spoke to him shortly after the worst storms for a

decade had ravaged the coast and caused flooding of
the small market towns inland. 'The rain was horizontal
and I could feel the whole house moving in the wind.'

Curiously, the front of the house faces inland,
towards a golf course, but the design is such that it
doesn't matter. 'It's very well designed. The front has
all the corridors, and the kitchen is at the front too.
The back is all windows looking out over the sea. It's
absolutely on the beach – the surf crashes at the end.
The drawing room has bay windows looking out at the
sea and there's a conservatory that's basically a
glassed-in veranda. It's a marvellous space all year
round and everyone spends all their time in there.'

The decor of the house is inspired by the light, the
sea and the shingle beach, which has heavy wooden
groynes marching far out into the water, built to
protect the coast from erosion. The rooms are full of
bits of worn driftwood and sea-washed ropes found
among the shingle; there are decoy ducks, shells and
sea-smoothed pebbles. Paintings – propped rather

than hung, to preserve the essential whiteness – refer
to yachts and lighthouses, brilliant blue coastal skies
and bright sands. Many of the objects are presents
from friends who can't resist the ambience. 'Pebbles
and shells work naturally down here – but I must try
not to buy any more lifebuoys and fishing nets. I've
got to be careful not to go over the top with it all. It's
a fine balance between the tasteful and kitsch.'

Sardinia is a favourite holiday spot. 'I love it and
go there for two weeks every year, staying in the
same house.' From the island come shells and twigs.
Two particularly clever wall lamps made of spiky twigs
(with electric wiring concealed in the centre of the
wood) are from the island, as is the clump of bleached
and twisted dried stems that sits in a shell-hung
pot – a white pot, of course. 'The house lends itself
to these bleached colours, to glass and steel. I find
it incredibly pleasing – perhaps because I don't like
things engineered and polished.'

David made a few economies in the house, although
they are not obvious. A 'pebble-dashed' fireplace was
plastered over and painted white. The kitchen, facing
the golf course, was made from Ikea units. Then he
found that the heavy wooden beams were, in fact,
made of polystyrene, so they had to go, while the
whole was given a Portland stone floor. To the outrage
of some conservationists, he replaced the original
bathroom with 'a very nice, very simple' alternative.

Indeed, simplicity is everything here, with the decor
being subordinated to the view and the sea. 'I believe
buildings have karma built into them for good or bad.

This is a very happy place. Waking up is amazing. The place is an ornithologist's dream, since the marshes nearby are a sanctuary for birds. The sounds they make are fascinating. Inland, nature tends to be hidden, but here it is always interesting, an experience. When it's hot, it's baking; when it's windy, it's really windy. I can't believe how harsh the winters can be – sometimes the plants in the garden are blown at 45 degrees and look quite dead. Then it all comes back in the spring.'

The planting is mostly of those Mediterranean species that can cope with wind, drought, salty air and sharp drainage. Rosemary, santolina, sage, some lavender, cardoons and tamarisk which, despite its delicate appearance, survives the storms.

Stephen Woodhams did little to change the overall formal design of the garden, 'although he did increase the size of the beds – they were rather mean'. But he imported quantities of seawashed pebbles, which alternate with the low plantings of santolina and purple sage in the beds – all protected from the elements by low woven-willow hurdles. Large terracotta pots with symmetrical box bushes lead the eye past a central urn laden with circular stones down to the stony beach itself. Seen from the upstairs windows, this formal arrangement with massive vernacular touches makes the perfect transition from the solidity of the house to the wilderness of the beach beyond.

picture credits

a=above, **b**=below, **r**=right, **l**=left, **c**=centre.

2 Alan & Diana Cardy's house in Sydney designed by The Cox Group; **4-5 & 6** Philip Cox's house in Palm Beach designed by The Cox Group; **7** Camp Kent designed by Alexandra Champalimaud; **9a & 9bl** Terry & Heather Dorrough's house on Dangar Island, New South Wales designed by Terry Dorrough Architect; **9br** Joan & Ben Francis–Jones' house in Woy Woy designed by Richard Francis–Jones; **10ar & 10b** Suzy & Graham Hurst's house in Palm Beach, Sydney, New South Wales; **15al** Alan & Diana Cardy's house in Sydney designed by The Cox Group; **16** main a house in Cape Elizabeth designed by Stephen Blatt Architects; **16** inset Peter & Tonia Tesorieros' apartment in Sydney designed by Alexander Tzannes Associates; **17a** photograph by Brian Leonard; **18-27** Fern Mallis' house in Southampton, Long Island; **28-35** compound by a lakeside in the mountains of western Maine designed by Stephen Blatt Architects; **36-43** Camp Kent designed by Alexandra Champalimaud; **44-49** a house in Maine designed by Stephen Blatt Architects; **52-59** Roderick & Gillie James' house in Devon designed by Roderick James Architects and built by Carpenter Oak & Woodland Co. Ltd; **60-65** Terry & Heather Dorroughs' house on Dangar Island, New South Wales designed by Terry Dorrough Architect; **66-71** Les Reedman's house on Dangar Island, New South Wales, Australia; **72-75** Rupert Morgan's barge in Paris; **76-79** a houseboat in Paris owned by a nature lover who wants to feel closer to the country; **80-81** Laurence & Yves Sabourets' house in Brittany; **82-85** Robert & Gabrielle Reeves' house in Clareville designed by Stutchbury & Pape Architecture + Landscape Architecture; **86-91** Philip Cox's house in Palm Beach designed by The Cox Group; **92-99** Laurence & Yves Sabourets' house in Brittany; **100-107** a house in Cape Elizabeth designed by Stephen Blatt Architects; **110-17** Elena Colombo's cottage on the east end of Long Island; **118-23** Waverley townhouse, Barbados, designed by Larry Warren; **124-33** Interior Designer Philip Hooper's own house in East Sussex; **134-39** David Davies' house in East Sussex, England.

The author and publisher would like to thank the people listed above for providing photographic locations.

business credits

Stephen Blatt Architects
10 Danforth Street
Portland
Maine 04101
USA
+ 1 207 761 5911
sba@sbarchitects.com
www.sbarchitects.com
Architectural design firm.
Pages **16 main**, **28–35**, **44–49**,
100–107.

Carpenter Oak Ltd
The Framing Yard
East Cornworthy
Totnes
Devon TQ9 7HF
01803 732 900
www.carpenteroak.com
Specialists in the construction of new oak-framed buildings and timber engineering.
Pages **52–59**.

Alexandra Champalimaud &
Associates Inc.
One Union Square West, # 3
New York
NY 10003
USA
+ 1 212 807 8869
www.alexchamp.com
Interior architecture and design.
Pages **7**, **36–43**.

The Cox Group
204 Clarence Street
Sydney 2000
Australia
+ 61 2 9267 9599
sydney@cox.com.au
www.cox.com.au
Architects and planners.
Pages **2**, **4–5**, **6**, **15al**, **86–91**.

Terry Dorrough Architect
14 Riverview Avenue
Dangar Island
NSW 2083
Australia
+ 61 2 9985 7729
Design of houses and small projects.
Pages **9a** & **9bl**, **60–65**.

Richard Francis-Jones
MGT Architects
Level 5
140 George Street
Sydney NSW 2000
Australia
+ 61 2 9251 7077
www.mgtarchitects.com
fjmt@fjmt.com.au
Multi-award-winning architects who have recently received Australia's highest award for excellence in the design of public buildings; they also undertake many residential projects.
Page **9br**.

Philip Hooper
Studio 30
The Old Latchmere School
38 Burns Road
London SW11 5GY
020 7978 6662
Interior designer.
Pages **124–33**.

Roderick James Architects
Seagull House
Dittisham Mill Creek
Dartmouth
Devon TQ6 0HZ
01803 722474
www.roderickjamesarchitects.com
An architectural practice specializing in contemporary wood and glass buildings.
Pages **52–59**.

Les Reedman
P.O. Box 148
Brooklyn
NSW 2083
Australia
+ 61 2 9985 7893
Chartered architect and architectural historian.
Pages **66–71**.

Stutchbury & Pape Architecture +
Landscape Architecture
4/364 Barrenjoey Road
Newport
NSW 2106
Australia
+ 61 2 9979 5030
snpala@ozemail.com.au
Have a reputation for innovative thinking and environmental sensitivity. The land, site and place are seen as directives towards the solution of formulating a building.
Pages **82–85**.

Alexander Tzannes Associates
Pty Limited
63 Myrtle Street
Chippendale
NSW 2008
Australia
+ 61 2 9319 3744
tzannes@tzannes.com.au
Architecture, interior design.
Pages **16** inset.

Larry Warren Architect
Derricks
St James
Barbados
+ 1 246 432 6392/2409
Pages **118–23**.

index